Cromosys Publication

ENGLISH WORD POWER

NIRANJAN JHA SHOWMAN

Founder - Niranjan Jha Showman

Education and Technology Research Center

Patankar Park, Nallasopara (W), Mumbai. +91-9561450045

Education, Technology, Publication, Healthcare, Newsmedia, Realtor, Filmmaking

www.facebook.com/cromosys

+91-9561450045
Learn Advanced Skills
And Get Job Instantly
GERMAN
Python
FRENCH
C++
SPANISH
Java
ENGLISH
HTML5
RUSSIAN
CSS
JavaScript
Cromosys
Education and Technology Research Center
Nallasopara (W), Mumbai

Learn Web Programming
Demo-Class Free
HTML
CSS
React
JavaScript
Typescript
Bootstrap
Cromosys
20 Years of Experience
Nallasopara (W), Mumbai
+91-9561450045

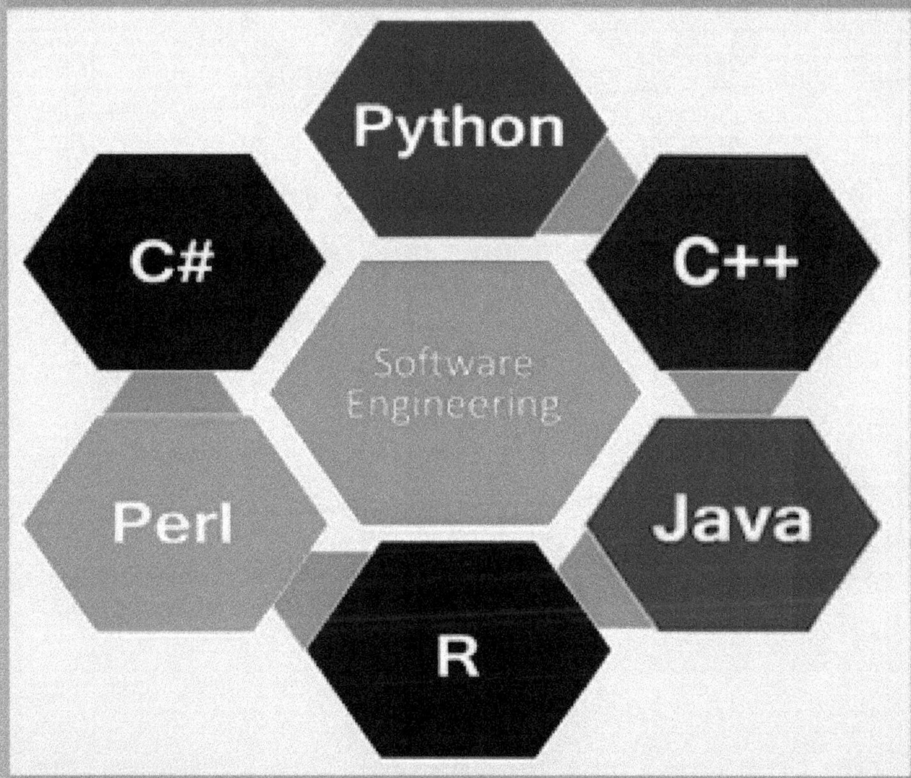
+91-9561450045
Learn Software Engineering
Demo-Class Free
Python
C#
C++
Software
Engineering
Perl
Java
R
Cromosys
20 Years of Experience
Nallasopara (W), Mumbai
+91-9561450045

25 Years of Experience
Learn Visual Multimedia
Animation VFX
Movie Editing
Game Development
Cromosys
+91-9561450045
Education and Technology Research Center
Nallasopara (W), Mumbai
www.facebook.com/cromosys

Jobs Available
For Candidates Who Know

German
French
Spanish

Vacancy in Germany, France, Spain

For Hospitality, Engineering, IT Sector
With Free Visa, Airfare and Accommodation

Cromosys
Education and Technology Research Centre
Nallasopara (W), Mumbai
+91-9561450045
20 Years of Experience

+91-9561450045
Foreign Languages Institute
German, French, Spanish
Basic and Advanced - All Levels
3 x 6 = 18 Courses
FRANCHISE
Business Offer
Teaching Materials Provided
We have 1 Million Students Globally
Great Income Assured
Global Exposure
Cromosys
20 Years of Experience
Nallasopara (W), Mumbai
+91-9561450045

Cromosys Publication

English Word Power

Niranjan Jha Showman

"Education taken with zeal educes to success."
~Niranjan Showman

Preface

Cromosys Publication's "English Word Power" book is an optimal quality guide to the beginners as well as advanced learners to increase the knowledge of English words. It is an unmatchable unique book of its kind that guarantees your success. The perfectly designed study materials based on my fifteen years of linguistic research are magnificently powerful to bring you into educational light. Since English is accepted as a global language, people around the world have been sharpening their knowledge to be good in it. Sometimes, only working knowledge of it doesn't work and you feel that there is a lot more to explore. The accurate and profound knowledge of this language, which was considered to be existing only in England and America in past, has influenced zillions of mind today, therefore I conceived the idea of making this book a guideline for those who want to be perfect in English.

The significance of this book is that it is dynamic, systemic and blissful with abundance of pre-existing and new words which are strong, vital and vivaciously meaningful taken from literature, psychology, theology, science, and technology. The reason why this book is so useful is that it has alphabetically listed more than three thousand words with their meanings written in the simplest way which you don't not find in other books. I have seen other word power books which the compilers or lexicographers have crammed up with obsolete, difficult and junk words because they think a word power book should have only difficult words in it. It is their biggest mistake. Moreover, they don't arrange the words in an order, so when you want to locate a word for second time, you have to start from the beginning again. That is why, taking all precautions, I've made this book simple and friendly to you.

The compilation of this book took a decade of that time during which I myself got into the language training in the USA and communicated with native English speakers around the world managing a team in several call centers. Additionally, I learnt French, Spanish, and German, and then studied at least five leading dictionaries and thesauruses such as Oxford, Cambridge and Webster. And after that, I studied all the three Holy Scriptures that includes The Geeta, The Bible, and The Quran. Thereafter, I got intuited to be able to understand linguistic science and compile this Word Power Book. This simple, sober and lovable book is designed with light-hearted and cheerful attempts to help people improve knowledge without falling into grandiloquence and unbearable rigidity of the language. It encourages reading considering it an essential human activity which seems to be deteriorating in the world day-by-day. It has been observed that other big-size importable dictionaries are always kept in cupboard for blue-moon reading, and cockroaches get enough of time to eat the pages. In order to make this book a little entertaining, the meaning of some words (not all) are written in metaphoric, idiomic or slangish sense ignoring any prejudiced, insular, orthodox, hypocrite views.

One alone, being immaturely suggested, spends ages in reading literature, watching movies and listening to the audio which help them to imitate a little but not gain the word power what in actual sense it is. And their never-ending process of Picasso Adventure collects some scattered information which is unworthy to linguistic approach. And as a result of shallow efforts, the aspirants get lost in wilderness. Whether you want to travel abroad or plunge deep into your research, your word power will build your caliber in writing, speaking and navigating around the world. With the growth of several call centers, there is a need of talented people to express clearly in the field of communication. The telecommunication industry has greatly inspired several people to have a neutral accent so that the communication should be more effective. This is a major advantage that will help you get a job.

Cromosys, our education and technology research center, saving human efforts from being wasted, is to make you as good as native English speaker. The world growing with density has brought enormous opportunity to linguistic talents irrespective of their geographical boundaries. Having been teaching English, French, Spanish, and German to global exposure for last thirteen years successfully, I have come across numerous amazingly beautiful and meaningful words which got their entry only in this book. I strongly believe it is useful for the people working for communication-based industry, media houses, entertainment world, and obviously for those who love English. It will stand a milestone for you in your journey and will help you sharpen your ability and make your way of success without any hindrance. As you are going to do the most beautiful thing for yourself, so be bold enough to go through this book completely. Cromosys, out education and technology research center, which is a path-breaking pioneer training institute for Spoken English, French, Spanish, German, and Computer Science, is committed to enlightening human mind with educational wisdom. And we are doing the same from last successful fifteen years. We not only hope but believe that your success is in your hand now, and this book will take you miles ahead in your expectation. We always respect the views and comments of readers. For any communication with regards to assistance, enquiry or collaboration, we are always at your reach as it helps us improve our ability.

Niranjan Jha Showman
Trainer, Author Physician, Entrepreneur, Filmmaker, Activist
Founder of Cromosys Corporation
facebook.com/cromosys
+91-9561450045
cromosys@yahoo.com
Nallasopara (W), Mumbai, India

My other books: -
English Voice Accent and Pronunciation
Teach Yourself German
Teach Yourself French
Teach Yourself Spanish
Be millionaire like me
Dynamic Grammar of English
Teach Yourself HTML5
Teach Yourself 3ds Max
Teach Yourself Autodesk Maya

Cromosys Corporation
Education and Technology Research Center
Education, Technology, Publication, Healthcare, Realtor, Filmmaking
facebook.com/cromosys
+91-9561450045
cromosys@yahoo.com
Nallasopara (W), Mumbai, India

About the Author

Niranjan Jha Showman
Trainer, Author, Physician, Entrepreneur, Filmmaker, Activist

Niranjan Jha Showman is a Language Scientist and Technical Researcher. He is the Award Winning author of more than fifty educational and fictional books at Amazon. He is one of the great-grandsons of the first President of India Dr. Rajendra Prasad. He is a Public Figure, and the globally - renowned Languages Trainer of French, Spanish, and German from past twenty years. Niranjan Jha Showman is an Entrepreneur and also works as a Filmmaker in India. Being the founder and owner of Cromosys Corporation - a company located in Mumbai, India, his company is excelling in the fields of Education, Technology, Publication, Newsmedia, Realtors, Banking, and Cinemascope from past fifteen years.

Niranjan Jha Showman's good-seller educational books and novels are appreciated worldwide. He has more than one million eBook buyers online, and more than one million learners are connected to him globally. One of his novels is critically acclaimed. He is the trainer of French, Spanish, German, English Voice and Accent, and Advanced Computer Education. He is also a political activist in India.

Niranjan Jha Showman is the man who came from rags to riches, he who knows how to turn the table, and he, whom you call the man of Midas-touch. He has observed lives from the Pandora of monkeys to the sanctuary of monks, not only down-to-earth but down-to-grave. He is a B. Com. graduate, and B. Ed. from Delhi University, and diploma holder in French, Spanish and German from America. You can watch his songs, movies, educational videos and many more things by typing "Niranjan Jha Showman" in Google.

Niranjan Jha Showman
+91-9561450045
cromosys@yahoo.com
Mumbai, India
facebook.com/cromosys

Statutory

This book with its content is the registered property of the author Niranjan Jha Showman.
The author and his Cromosys Publication holds all necessary rights of this book.
The copyright certificate of this book is attached at the end of this book.

This book is a copyright and its content is the registered property of the author Niranjan Jha Showman. The author and his Cromosys Publication holds all necessary rights of this book. All the writing works that include all the educational, non-educational books, novels, and articles of the writer Niranjan Jha Showman, are the registered content under MAHENG12112/13/1/2009-TC and the endorsement no. 3244 28/5/2009 with the Ministry of Information and Broadcasting, Govt. of India. Any plagiarism in this regard will attract strict legal action. Any further publication or production of any of his books requires his written permission. The copyright certificate of this book is attached at the end of this book.

A

Abattoir: A building or place used for the killing of animals for human food. In metaphoric sense, this word is used for the place where a large number of people are killed

Abbevillian: The old culture when people were leading uncivilized life

ABC sex: Sex only on anniversaries, birthdays and Christmas

Abnormalism: The thinking that the world is an abnormal place and nothing is good and systematic here in it

Abolitionist: A person involved in the activity of ending any custom, institution or a law

Abrasive: The one who is very rude because he has no manner

Absconder: A man who runs away unlawfully because he has done something wrong and doesn't want to be caught

Absent minded: A person who frequently forgets the things because of weak memory

Abstainer: One who keeps himself under control and does not drink alcohol or consume narcotic things

Absurdism: The thinking that the world is useless and human life is futile

Access course: The course that enables a person to get direct admission in a college without formal education

Accident: A child whose conception was not planned by their parents

AC-DC: A man who is sexually attracted by the persons of either sex, also called 'ambisextrous', bisexual

Ace boon: A best friend of yours

Achilles' heel: Your weak point or bad quality that you think the people can take advantage of or harm you. (Pronunciation – *akileez heel*)

Acid house: A place where people take drugs

Acid test: A severe test that you apply to examine or find out the truth of something

Acquaintance rape: The rape in which the persons involved are familiar to the victim

Action duplex: A sexual act involving both vaginal and anal sex

Action gagnée: A successful and joyful sexual intercourse (Pronounced – action gagnee)

Action station: A place where the soldiers take position to start attacking on their enemies

Activist: A very active member of any political party or social group

Acushla: A female partner of a man who he loves very much, (Pronounced *akyushla*)

Adam's apple: A ball type projection at the front and in the middle of the neck of a young male person

Adam teasing: An act of a female person intending to harass a man

Adulterer: A man or woman who commits a sexual act with the person who is not married to him or her

Adventurous: A person who has a tendency of taking high risk

Affable: A person with good nature and behavior

Affiliation order: A legal order of the court to the man when he is found the father of an illegally born child, to help and support the child

Afroginist: The black people from African origin who support back-racism and contradict Zionist attitude in America [Blend of Afro and originist]

After life: The life that one is supposed to get after death

After pain: The pain that a mother bears while delivering a child

Afterthought: The younger child in a family who is born considerably later than the other children

After world: The world after death

Agent provocateur: A person employed in police or anti-crime department who tempts a suspected criminal to do crime so that he can be arrested

Age of consent: The age when a person can have sex

Aggrandizer: A deeply involved man in increasing his power, rank, or wealth

Aggressive: A person with forceful and hostile nature who tries to pressurize others for his decisions

Agnostic: If you believe that the world cannot ever know anything about God, then you are an agnostic

Agony ant: A person who gives personal advices to the readers by writing in the newspaper for their problems

Agoraphobe: A person with the fear of public speaking

Air jerk: Making a motion with hands to express disgust, disinterest or disbelief while rolling eyes

Airlocked: Drunk, intoxicated

Alaskan Firedragon: A sexual activity in which a man ejaculates on the face of his partner

Alexia: A mental disability when a person is not able to concentrate in reading or study

Algolegnia: The vaginal pain during sexual intercourse

Alimony: The money that a man pays to his wife or ex after separation

Alislut: A woman who has the intention of getting married to a rich man and then seeking divorce to accumulate money [Contraction of alimony and slut]

Alley cat: A prostitute who keeps roaming around the streets frequently

Alligator: A fan of jazz or swing music

Alltheist: A person with such a broad spiritual views that he respects all the religions

Alpha dog: A head of the family who dominates his family members

Alpha geek: The most technically proficient and knowledgeable member of a group

Altar tapism: 1.The selfish motive of some religious people to occupy the entire world. 2. The tendency of some religious people to use their shrine for their own gratification

Amazon: A tall, beautiful, and well-built athletic woman

Ambiguous: A sentence with no clear meaning

Ambisextrous: A man who is sexually attracted by the persons of either sex

Ambivert: If you are neither too much willing to mix around nor keeping yourself very much reserved, which means you are balancing a state between extroversion and introversion, then you are ambivert

Ambulance chaser: The one who takes benefits from others' misfortune

American dream: Your dream to bring equality, democracy and prosperity in your country

Anarchy: A condition when the government is having no control on the people, and it has caused a great political or social disorder (Pronunciation – *anərki*)

Ancestor: The member of your past generation

Anilingus: The sexual act of licking or kissing the anus

Ankle biter: A young child who disturbs his parent for small things

Annihilation: A complete destruction of something

Anork: A person who is absurd and unfashionable by his nature

Anorexia: A psychological illness when you refuse eating in order to lose your weight

Antenuptial contract: The terms and conditions that is fixed between a man and woman before they are going to marry

Antidote: A medicine given to a patient to remove the poison from the body

Antwacky: Old fashioned (Pronounced – aantwaki)

Ape: A sexually aggressive man

Aphasia: An abnormal mental condition when a person is not able to understand or speak anything

Aphrodisiac: The medicine that increases excessive sexual desire

Apocalypse: Great or total destruction

Apostate: A man who doesn't believe in his religion

Apple polisher: A person who treats others with special kindness so that he can get help

Apprentice: The one who is learning their work being employed for a period at a low salary

Arbiter: A person appointed to work as a mediator to settle a dispute

Archaist: The one who thinks that old culture was good and the people of today should follow that

Arch enemy: The uncompromising enemy who wants to kill you at any cost

Arch-slave: The woman in religious service who is being sexually exploited by their male leaders

Argot: The code-language that a group or class uses in criminal activities

Argument from design: A religious belief that the nature is designed in such way that proves the existence of God

Aristocratism: The doctrine in India to defeat communism and its radical naxal activities

Arm candy: Arm candy: A physically attractive companion who is working as a bodyguard or escort to a celebrity or influential person

Aristocracy: The government formed by the rich people of the society

Arriviste: A very ambitious and too much selfish person

Arse-licker: A sycophant who treats others with special kindness so that he can get help

Arse-man: A man whose favorite part of a woman's anatomy is the buttocks

Articulate: A person who is able to speak his language fluently and nicely

Artificial insemination: The semen injection given to a woman to get pregnant

Aastala vista: See you again, good bye (Spanish word)

Ascetic: Someone who does not involve in any kind of pleasure by keeping himself under severe self-discipline for religious reason

Askhole: Someone who asks many stupid, pointless, and obnoxious questions

Assassin: The one who kills a politician or religious leader

Ass bandit: A man more inclined to have anal sex than vaginal, also called 'sodomite'

Ass chaser: A man looking for news girls to go bed with

Asset beauty: A beautiful woman with good-shaped buttocks

Assignation: A secret meeting of two lovers considered illicit by the society

Asylum: A place where mentally ill or distressed people are kept for proper treatment and care

Atheism: The belief that God does not exist

Attendance center: A place where a child, who has committed a crime, is kept for minor penalty

Attitudinizer: Someone who is very good in peaking and behavior

Audiophile: A person who always likes to be in happy mood

Aunt flow: Menstruation

Aura: A supposed light surrounding the body of a living mystic or spiritual person

Aussie kiss: An act of kissing or licking sexual organs, also called 'blow job, cunnilingus, fellatio, carpet munching'

Autocracy: A government by one person ruling over a country

Autocue: The monitor that displays the hints for a newsreader for a television program

Autodidact: A person who has learnt the things on his own without any formal education

Avaricious: Someone who is greedy of accumulating more and more money

Avocation: A secondary profession

B

Babbler: Someone who talks too much and opens some secrets which he should not do

Babe magnet: A male person who is very smart in attracting girls

Babia-majora: An extremely attractive woman

Bachelorette: A single British woman

Back bencher: The student who sits at the back in a classroom

Back bitter: A person who speaks something bad about you in your absence

Backdoor: To commit adultery with (verb)

Back-fire: The situation when you are expecting some good result from the work you are doing, but something opposite and dangerous happens

Backhander: A bribe or secret payment made to gain some benefits

Back passage: Anus

Backroom boys: The people who do important work for a person or an organization but the public do not know about them

Back slang: The language spoken using the words or letters backwards, like – instead of '*boy*' you speak '*yob*'

Backsnurging: The act of sexual pleasure when a man sniffs or smells female underwear

Backseat driver: The one who is too eager to advise others without responsibility

Backstreet boy: A boy involved in some illegal activities

Backy Fiona: A girl who has well-grown and round buttock which makes her look beautiful and attractive

Bad blood: The enmity between two persons

Bad debt: The money that you have given to somebody as a debt but there is no chance that he will pay you back

Bad hair day: A day when you feel that everything is going wrong with you and that is making you upset and annoyed

Bad paymaster: Your boss who does not pay your salary on time or unreasonably cuts it

Bahaism: A religion that is divided from Islam and founded in 1863 in Iran, which believes in one God and emphasizes the unity of all the religions

Bad-mouth: To criticize (verb)

Bail bandit: Someone who commits a crime while on bait awaiting a trial

Balderdash: Nonsense

Ball and chain: A man's wife

Bald-headed hermit: The penis

Ballsy: The one who is courageous and powerful

Banana republic: A country with weak government unable to maintain the rule and regulation

Banker's ramp: A conspiracy by bankers to engineer a financial crisis in order to damage the standing of a government to which they are inimical

Barbie doll: A beautiful, sexy but characterless young woman

Barebacking: Anal sex without condom

Barren: A woman who is not able to give birth to a child

Basket: A child who is born to unmarried parents

Basket case: A country which is in bad economical condition with no possibility to come up

Bawd: A woman who runs a prostitute house and collects the money from the clients coming in

Bazookas: The large breasts of a woman

Battleaxe: A domineering woman

B-boy: A participant in hip hop street culture

Beach-bum: A person devoted to spending as much time as available on the beach

Beam-scream struggle: The very rigorous struggle that you do to grow in life

Beanpole: A very tall thin person

Beauty sleep: The sleep that you get before midnight

Beaver: The female sexual organ and surrounding area

Bed of honor: The grave of a soldier died fighting for his country

Bedroom eyes: The way of looking at someone with the intention of having physical relation (Noun)

Bed wetter: A child who urinates in bed while sleeping

Beer belly: A punch developed by drinking large quantities of beer

Beer goggles: The effect of alcohol when one finds others more sexually attractive (Noun)

Beestings: The thick and yellow color first milk of the mother fed to the new born baby

Bejesus: Expressing surprise or annoyance

Belly button: The navel

Belly-laugh: A deep uncontrollable laugh

Beltway bandit: A private company that hires a person who was previously employed in government agencies, so that the company can get some government contacts

Benchmark: A standard of something which can be used to compare other

Benefactor: A person or an organization who gives money and other help to you

Benevolent: A person who actively helps you with genuine heart without any kind of bad motive or seeking anything in return from you

Benign: Someone who is gentle and kind hearted

Bestiality: A person's sexual involvement with animals

Betrothal: A promise or agreement to marry

Bevvy: A general term for an alcoholic drink

B girl: A woman employed at shop to encourage customers to buy more

Bible basher: The one who speaks a lot about the Bible or Christianity

Bibliophile: Someone who loves reading books

Bible pounder: A person who follows the instructions of the Bible in a vigorous and aggressive manner

Bigamy: The crime of marrying a second time when you are already married

Big bucket: A woman who looks ugly because of her exceptionally big buttock

Big-mouth sister: If a man calls a woman his sister just to show to the people but goes in physical relation with her, so that woman is his 'big-mouth sister'

Big Apple: New York City

Big girl's blouse: A man with no physical strength

Bigot: A person who is obstinate and not ready to tolerate anything happening against his belief, religion or political theory

Billy no-mates: A person who has no friend

Bimbo: A woman who is young and beautiful but behaves like a child

Biological father: When a woman gets pregnant by the injected sperm of a man and delivers a child, that man is called biological father of the child

Bitch slap: A stinging slap or blow to humiliate someone

Blabbermouth: A speaker who reveals too much

Black bomber: The drug to stimulate for sex

Black hole: The mistake one commits by not meeting the quality parameter in service

Black Maria: A police vehicle that is used for transporting prisoners

Black Mass: The activity of worshiping a devil in black church by playing loud music and naked dance giving immoral presentation of Roman Catholic Religion

Black spot: A place on the road where accidents may take place

Black velvet: An attractive woman of black color

Blagger: Someone who persuades or agitates other in such a way that he can get benefits

Blasphemy: A talk or writing something bad about God or religion

Bleaker: The parents, especially a father who persuades his daughters to become a call-girl

Bleeding heart: A very soft-hearted and sensitive person who uncontrollably over-reacts if something unpleasant happens to him

Blind man's buff: A game played by the children when one child's eyes are covered so that he can not see, and then he has to touch other players

Bliss: A perfect joy with extreme happiness

Bloated: Someone who is so proud of his richness that he behaves rudely

Blockfig: Your girlfriend's lover [Contraction of blocking figure]

Blood bath: The killing of a large number of people

Blood money: The money that is paid to kill somebody

Blooming lunatic: A highly educated but stupid person

Blop strop: The tension of a woman related to her menstruation problem

Blow job: Fellatio or cunnilingus that involves kissing and licking of sexual organs

Blue ball: The extreme sexual frustration of a man (Noun)

Blue beard: A man who kills his wife

Blue blank: The depression causing madness

Blue blooded: Someone who is from a royal or noble family

Blue-carpet boss: A boss who persuades his female employees for lovemaking

Blue-chip investment: The investment that you think is safe and will make a profit

Blue-collar job: A labor-class job that is done with physical effort

Blue funk: Your mental state when you feel extreme fear or terror

Blue-eyed boy: Your favorite person whom you treat with special favor

Blue-line bonker: A man inclined to make love to very young girls of his age

Blue waffles: A severe infection on the vagina with too much of burning because of excessive intercourse

Blue-grapes: The physical relation between a husband and wife occurring very rarely because of lack of interest, in sentence: *He is giving me some blue-grapes, nothing else.*

Blue slave: A woman who works in a hotel as a waitress cum prostitute

Bluestocking: A well-educated woman, who is more interested in ideas and studying than in traditional old fashioned things related to woman only

Blunt: A cigar whose wrapper has been emptied of tobacco and filled with marijuana

Bobfoc: A female with attractive body but ugly face (Pronounced – bobfok)

Body double: A duplicate actor who works in films at the place of a real actor for some nude or offensive scenes

Bohemian: Someone who lives in a free and informal way because he doesn't like accepted rules of society

Bomb shell: A very attractive and sexy woman

Bone-belt: A black magician seeking sexual favor from his female followers

Bonkbuster: A book or film characterized by frequent sexual encounters between the characters

Booby prize: A prize given to a person who is last in a competition

Booby rampage: The sexual activity of a woman rubbing her breasts with male genital, also called 'Dutch sex'

Boon companion: A good friend of yours who is very helpful to you

Booty bandit: A man who commits male rape

Booty grazing: The act of sending one message to many people at a time in hopes that a guaranteed physical relation for the night will be established

Bosom friend: A very close friend of yours

Bosomy: A woman who looks very attractive because of her large breasts

Botch job: A makeshift construction or repair of something that is going to fail in a long run

Bottler: The one who easily gives up or loses his courage to complete a task

Bottle shouldered: A person whose shoulder is not straight

Bottom drawer: The asset that a girl keeps before marriage for her husband or his family

Bouncer: Someone employed in a club or meeting place whose duty is to throw out the person who troubles others

Bounty hunter: A person who pursues a criminal to get him arrested so that he can get a reward

Box and cox: The two persons who share only one room and use it at a different time

Boyfriend drop: When you propose a girl but she refuses telling a lie to you that she already has a boyfriend, so this activity of her is called 'boyfriend drop'

Bracket busy: A mentally upset or frustrated person who pretends to be busy but the fact is that he has lost his interest to do any work

Brain drain: The movement when the highly qualified and intelligent people of their own country go to some other country to live better lives

Brainiac: Very intelligent person

Brain storm: A mental disturbance that is so violent that you are not able to control yourself

Brass monkey weather: Extremely cold weather

Brat pack: A group of film stars enjoying a rowdy or fun-loving lifestyle

Brazilian cold: A mental disorder in which you feel very annoyed when somebody reminds you something unpleasant

Bread basket: Stomach

Breadhead: A person who is obsessed with making money

Bread winner: The person who supports his family with the money he earns

Breathalyzer: A device used by the police to measure the amount of alcohol in a driver's breath

Breech birth: A birth in which the baby's feet come out first which is a little risky for the life of the baby or the mother

Brewer's droop: A temporary impotence as a result of drinking excessive amount of alcohol

Broken mirror: 1.A superstition or blind belief which is still being followed by the people 2. Poverty

Broken-mirror stress: The heavy stress of extreme poverty (Noun)

Brothel: A place like an apartment where the prostitutes call their clients, also called bordello

Brother of broadway: A man who behaves decently showing brotherly affection to a woman but his true intention is to develop romantic relationship

Brouhaha: A useless commotion

Brown-collar job: The job of a soldier

Brown envelop: The thing that is full of confusion

Brown-nose: The one who praise other or behave sycophantically

Brunch: The food that you eat in the late morning as a combination of breakfast and lunch

Bubblehead: An empty headed and stupid person

Buffer guest: A friend of yours who you call in a party just to show to the other guests that the party is already started when they come

Buffoon: Someone who does silly things and because of that other people feel amused

Bugger: An anal sex lover

Bull-dyke: A lesbian with masculine tendencies

Bull's eye: The center point of your target that you want to shoot

Bum-bag: A small pouch worn around the waist or hips, held in place by a strap or belt, and used to hold valuables and money

Bum-boy: A male prostitute

Bum-chum: A person with an apparently overly close friendship

Bumshot: Anal sex

Bunker sheltering: The activity of press media when they take bribes from a criminal and protect him by publicizing him innocent

Bunny-boiler: A jealous or obsessive woman whose behavior with her former or intended partner is desperate or dangerous

Bureaucracy: The system of official rules of a government or an organization which is so complicated for the people that they feel it is difficult to follow

Business magnate: A highly successful businessman

Busman's holiday: The holiday that you spent doing the same thing that you do at your work place

Busy body: The person who is too interested to know what other people are doing and tries to interfere

Butt crack: The upper part of a woman's buttock that is visible when she bends down because she has worn low-waist and skin-tight clothes

Butter-and-egg man: A wealthy unsophisticated man who spends money freely

Butterfly mind: The one who is very unstable with his thoughts and future plans and so he keeps on changing his mind

Butler English: Speaking English with fluency but lots of grammatical mistakes

Butter finger: A person who is so careless that he easily he drops the things from his hand

Buttock watch: The man who is too eager to look at the buttocks of a woman

Butt pirate: A male homosexual who enjoys sodomy

Button man: Someone who is working for a big criminal or underworld man at a low level

Buy-curious: The one who just looks at a shop but doesn't buy anything

By blow: The child who is born to unmarried parents

Bye law: The law that is made by a local authority and applies only to that area

C

Calf love: The love of adolescence age

Caliber: The quality or power of your character

California roll: When you fail to make a complete stop at a red light or stop sign especially at a turn

Camcouple: A married couple who captures the video of their own sexual act to sell online [Contraction of camera-couple]

Camel toe: When a woman is wearing a tight clothe and the front part of thighs and vaginal area appears to be mounding even if they are covered, that is called a 'camel toe'

Cannibal: A human flesh eater

Capital crime: A big crime which attracts death punishment

Caps lock voice: When a normally calm person raises his voice and uses an authoritative tone – that is called caps lock voice

Captious: A person who always tries to find bad things in other persons

Careerist: Someone who considers his career is more important than anything else

Carnage: The killing of a large number of people in a communal or other conflict

Carouse: The parties in which people spend time drinking, laughing and enjoying in a noisy way

Carsick: A person who vomits while traveling in a vehicle

Casanova: A very clever man who is tactful in managing with many girlfriends

Casting couch: A man working for a movie seeking sexual favor from his female associates

Casting vote: A deciding vote given by the chairperson when the votes on two sides are equal

Castrate: To remove the testicles of a male person or animal (Verb)

Casuist: A person who solves moral or legal problems by using clever arguments even if they are false

Catamite: A passive male homosexual partner

Catastrophe: A total destruction which may cause many or all the people to suffer or lose their lives

Catbird seat: A superior or advantageous position

Catch-22: A difficult situation when you are not able to escape because you have got two works to do and neither you can do both of the works at once, nor first work before doing second, nor second work before doing first

Catch phrase: A word or a sentence that you use quite often while speaking to somebody

Celibate: The one who refrains from sexual relation

Cesspool: A place where dishonest and immoral people gather

Chancer: The one who takes chances or does risky things

Chaos: A state or a condition of complete confusion and disorder

Character assassination: The act of somebody when he blames you for something you haven't done

Chastity belt: A belt worn by some religious women in past to protect virginity

Chequebook journalism: The activity of press and media house when they desperately look for hot news and they buy it by paying money

Chasy belt: A woman who has a very strong ill-feeling for sex, and so, she cannot allow a man to go physical with her [Colloquial of chastity belt]

Chauvinist: A person who believes and advocates that men are more important and intelligent than women (Pronunciation – *shauvinist*)

Checkmate: A position in the game of chess when one player cannot save his king because the important place is captured by other player

Chicken hearted: A weak hearted person lacking courage or confidence

Chick magnet: A male person very smart in attracting girls

Chick: A young woman, also called a chicklet

Chick flick: A film full of girls' poses

Child molester: A male person who has sex with small children

Chinaman's chance: A negligible prospect

Chinese whisper: The situation when the information is passed from one person to another but it gets slightly changed each time

Chinese angle: A strange or unusual twist or aspect to something

Chinless wonder: A rich person who lacks depth of character and intelligence

Chirology: The language of dumb people using their hands and fingers for communication

Christer: An over-religious person

Chopsocky: A kind of film featuring violent actions involving martial art

Chronoptimist: A person who always underestimates the time necessary to do something

Chubby-chaser: A person who finds fat people attractive

Church mouse: A very poor person who begs for living

Ciao: An Italian word used as a greeting at the time of meeting or departing (Pronunciation – chaao)

Cinephile: Someone who is very fond of watching movies

Circular problem: A set of many problems that you cannot get out of because each problem is the cause of one another

Circumlocution: The way when you are speaking or writing something not in a direct way and for that you use more words than necessary

Circumcise: To remove the loose piece of skin that covers the opening of a man's penis (Verb)

Circumspect: A person who is alert and careful about the things happening around him

City slicker: Someone who behaves in a way which is typically city-lifestyle

Civic center: An area in a town where municipal offices and other public buildings are situated

Civil war: A war when the people of the same country fight with each other

Cleanskin: Someone with a clean police record

Clean sneak: An escape with no clues left behind

Cleavage: The cut of a woman's upper clothe, which is revealing the space between her breasts

Clever-clogs: An idiot who claims to be clever or have great knowledge, also called 'clever Dick'

Clip-joint: A place of deception

Clippie: A female bus conductor

Clit: The small sensitive organ just above the opening of vagina which becomes larger when the woman is sexually excited

Cloth-ears: The one who has a poor sense of hearing

Clusterfuck: When a lot of things are going extremely wrong in a short period of time

Clustering: A sexual activity involving three persons, also called sandwich sex

Cockpit crunch: A sexual act when there is no appropriate time or place and that makes the situation a little fearful

Cocksman: A man who is considered to be exceptionally skilled in lovemaking

Cock-teaser: A sexually provocative woman, who attracts a man but refuses intercourse at the end, also called 'vagina drop'

Code brown: The condition when your stomach is upset and you are going to toilet again and again, also termed 'Delhi belly'

Cohabitation: The relationship between a man and woman when they are living together without being married

Coitus interruptus: An act of sexual intercourse when a man withdraws his penis before ejaculation to prevent pregnancy, (Pronunciation – *koitas intarapts*)

Cold courage: An advice that is not true but you are giving to someone to console him so that he can come out of the grief

Coldfish: An unemotional or insensitive person

Cold hearted: A person who lacks the feeling of love, courage, or sympathy for others

Cold reception: When somebody welcomes you showing happiness but in fact he is not happy and wants you to go as soon as possible, that is – cold reception

Cold sweat: The sweat that comes out of body when you are frightened of something very badly

Cold war: A very unfriendly relationship between two countries when they are not fighting but trying to harm each other by other means

Cold turkey: A bad condition of mind when someone feels that his body is shivering and mind is not stable at the time when he has suddenly stopped taking drugs

Collaborative: The person who wants all the people to grow and get success because he is not competing with anyone

Columbia shock: A very disturbing feeling perceived by a young man who visits a brothel for the first time and that results no erection on him

Come: The ejaculated semen

Come-on: The signal that a girl can give to encourage someone for lovemaking

Comedy of manners: The behavior of some people when they intend to show that they are happy and they try to make other also happy

Comfort station: The Toilet

Commandment: A law given to human being by God

Compassionate leave: A leave that somebody gets when someone has died at his place

Con artist: A cheater

Conceptus: A very new embryo

Concrete jungle: A city which has many large modern buildings and no trees or parks

Concubine: A woman who is living with a married man without marriage

Confidence trick: An act of cheating someone keeping him under confidence

Confinement: The time of a child's birth

Conjecture: An opinion or idea that is not based on definite knowledge but formed by guessing only

Considerate: A person who is wise and has good understanding power

Conspicuous consumption: The way of showing richness when one buys expensive things and shows them to the people

Coquette: A beautiful woman who behaves in a way that can easily attract a man (Pronunciation – *koket*)

Costa del Crime: A place where many fugitive criminals live

Co-respondent: A person who is having sexual relation with the wife or husband of somebody who is trying to get divorce

Core time: The central part of the working day when all the employees must be present

Coroner: An officer who is investigating on a murder case

Corporal punishment: The punishment that a person gives to himself by beating or causing injury considering that to be his religious duty

Cosmology: The science of the origin and development of the universe

Cosmopolitan: A person who is free from national limitations and religious belief because he thinks that all the nations are equal and all the religions are same

Cottage industry: A business that you are doing from your home

Couch potato: A person who likes wasting time by sitting at home and watching television

Counsel of despair: An action which you take at the end when all your previous efforts have failed

Counter culture: The way of life which is totally opposite to what the people believe is normal

Courtesan: A prostitute who is very famous because she has rich and upper class customers

Covenant: According to the Bible, the agreement between God and the people of Israel

Cowboy: Someone who is careless and dishonest in his work

Cowboy job: The activity of secretly getting important political or military information about another country or finding out another company's secrets by using spies

Coxcomb: A very proud and over-confident person

Coyote: An illegal agent who offer to send the people to America or any country but cheat them

Crabby: A moody and short tempered person

Crackpot: An impractical person in his behavior because he has some strange and crazy ideas

Cracksman: A thief

Cradle-snatcher: A man who likes to have sex with those who are quite younger than his age

Crapulent: Someone who drinks too much of alcohol

Crash pad: A place for the poor people to sleep

Crawler: A man who tries to get somebody's favor by praising him or doing all that will make him happy

Creationism: The belief that the universe and living organisms are originated from specific acts of divine Creation rather than by natural processes

Credential: The proof of your quality, experience, or achievement

Credibility gap: When you do not do what other people were expecting or you do exactly opposite to what you had said or promised before

Credulous: Someone who believes very easily because he is not so strong in his judgment

Creep-house: A brothel or other place where prostitutes rob their clients

Creeping Jesus: A person who shows to others that he is very religious but in fact he is not

Crestfallen: The man who has lost his belief or reputation in the eyes of the people known to him

Crime passiounel: The crime done in sexual jealousy

Crook: Dishonest or criminal minded

Crumb: A person who does not agree with others' opinion that is why he objects all the time

Crusade: The war that was fought in Palestine by European Christians and the Muslims in the middle ages

Cubicle coma: When you wake up you feel energized, but when you go to office, a wave of tiredness runs over you, and once you leave your office, you suddenly feel energized and everything seems to be ok – that is called cubicle coma

Cubicle monkey: A desk-bound officer who works too much in his office

Cuckold: 1 A man who likes to see his wife having sex with another man. 2 A man who is the husband of a prostitute

Cugar: An old woman looking for a younger boyfriend

Cugine: A young man taking initial steps to get into underworld (Pronounced kyugeen)

Cuisine: The method of cooking (Pronunciation – *kwizeen*)

Culchie: A rural dweller

Cult: A system of religious worship according to what is expressed in ritual

Cum droplet: The semen that a male partner ejaculates on the face of his partner

Cunnilingus: The sexual activity when a man kisses or licks the vagina of his female partner

Cunt: Female sexual organ

Cunt-struck: A man who is extremely infatuated with a woman

Cupboard love: The love between two people when they want to gain something because of selfish motives

Curate's egg: A thing that is partly good and partly bad

Curtain lecture: The shouting of a wife to her husband making sure others should not listen to it

Cut-out: A person who is acting as a mediator in the activity of secretly getting important political or military information about another country or finding out another company's secrets by using spies

Cut-throat competition: A very challenging competition

Cyberpunk: A young person who is very fond of using internet, computing and information technology

Cynic: Someone who does not believe in humanity and he hates all

Cynosure: The center part of a thing which is the object of attraction or admiration

D

Dab hand: A man very good at doing something because he is efficient and well-trained on that

Daisy chain: A sexual activity involving three people, also termed 'threesome'

Dalliance: A relationship between two persons that is not serious and that results a casual love affair

Damnation: The punishment to remain in hell

Damp: A man who easily ejaculates seeing beautiful woman because of his weak sexual power

Damp squib: An unsuccessful attempt of yours when you try to impress someone

Dandy: A man who is unnecessarily devoted to style, smartness and fashion

Darby and Joan: A married couple who is old but still loves each

Dark horse: An unpopular person who suddenly becomes famous because of getting success from an unexpected work done by him

Daredevil: Someone who enjoys doing dangerous thing in a way that other people may think is stupid

Dark lore: The knowledge or learning related to black magic

Date rape: The crime of raping a girl when the lover calls her on a date

Dating agency: A business center or an organization that arranges meeting between a man and a woman who want to begin a romantic relationship

Dazzle: To impress a person with knowledge or ability or any brilliant display or prospect

Dear John letter: The letter that a woman gives to a man terminating relationship (Noun – *Is she going to give you a Dear John letter?*)

Debauchee: Someone who is immoral in his sexual behavior (Pronounced – *dibauchee*)

Debonair: A fashionable and confident man

Deb's delight: An attractive young man in high society

Decadent: The person who shows low moral standard and has interest only in pleasure and enjoyment rather than serious things

Decollete: The top edge of a woman's dress that is designed to be very low in order to show her shoulders

Defeatist: Someone who thinks that he can not succeed in the work he is doing because he has very less confidence

Déjà vu: When you feel that you have previously experienced something which is happening to you now

Delhi belly: An upset stomach compelling you to go to toilet again and again

DT: A physical condition in which people who drink too much alcohol feel their body shaking and imagine they are seeing things which are really not there. (Abbreviation of delirium tremens)

Delusion: A false belief or opinion about yourself or your situation

Delusion of grandeur: A belief that you are more important than you actually think about yourself

Demagogue: A political leader who tries to win support by using arguments or rising issues which are very sensitive to religious or emotional view points

Deadpan: A person with no expression or emotion on his face

Death rattle: A gurgling sound that comes out of the throat of a dying person

Debt bored: Someone who is so bored with life that he just spends money to make it more exciting

Decadence: A moral or cultural fall after a person reaches to the peak of achievement

Decree absolute: The final order for divorce

Defamation: An attack on the good reputation of someone

Deficiency disease: A disease caused by the lack of some essential element in the diet

Delinquent: A person showing the tendency to commit crime

Deliverance: The final release from rebirth

Demigod: A being which is not fully but partly divine

Demonolatry: The worship of demons

Demonomania: An abnormal mental state in which a person thinks or behaves like he has got an evil spirit on him

Derelict: Someone who does not have his home or job or even property

Dervish: A person, especially a Muslim, who is inclined to live in poverty and austerity

Desk rage: The peak of office employees' stress level

Desperado: A person who does dangerous and criminal things without caring for himself or other

Desperate soul: A person who is restless and tensed because he is in the need of something and for that he is bothering others

Destitute: The man who has no food and shelter

Detention center: A place where the children those who have committed crime are kept for the brief detention

Deviant: A man with sexually abnormal behavior

Dewy-eyed: A very sentimental person who cries quite often

Dialectical materialism: The Marxist theory that political and historical events are due to a conflict of social forces caused by man's material needs

Dialectician: A person skilled in the art of investigating the truth of opinions related to metaphysical contradictions and their solutions

Dictator: A ruler who has a complete power over a country

Diehard: A very persistent and stubborn person

Dildo: An object shaped like a penis used for sexual pleasure

Dilemma: A situation in which you are confused because you are not able to decide which of two works you should do first

Dinky: A professional working couple who have no children

Dipsomania: An abnormal desire of drinking a lot of alcohol

Dirty weekend: A weekend that you spend secretly with your lover

Discussion Uganda: A discusses or talks about sex. In sentence – *What the discussion Uganda is going on there?*

Disgawsome: Something which is disgustingly awesome [Contraction of disgustingly awesome]

Disorderly house: A brothel

Displaced anger: When you are angry for some other reason but showing anger on someone or something else

Dissuader: A person who is very smart to divert your mind in such a way that you will drop the idea of doing the work that you had planned to do

Diversionist: Someone who believes that the ruling government should change for the betterment of the people

Divine intervention: An incident that makes you thing God has done something

D-notice: A government notice to news editors not to publish items on specified subjects for security reasons. (Abbreviation of defense notice)

Doggy bag: A bag given to a customer in a restaurant to put the leftovers food in it for home

Do-gooder: A well-meaning but unrealistic reformer

Dog's age: A long time. In sentence – *A dog's age has passed since I have seen you.*

Dogwatch: A night shift job especially in a newspaper office

Dolce vita: A life of pleasure and luxury

Doldrums: A period of inactivity or feeling of boredom and depression

Domino effect: The effect when one event causes a sequence of similar events

Dona: A man's sweetheart

Dooms day: The last day of the world when all will die

Dopester: The one who collects information and forecasts the result of a sport, election, etc.

Dot-com dick: Someone who keeps on browsing lot of websites on internet

Double bluff: The truth that somebody spoke to you in such a cunning and persuasive way that you took as a lie but in fact that is truth

Double-cross: An act of deceiving somebody showing that you are helping him

Double Dutch: The language that you can not understand at all

Double faced: Someone who admires you in your presence and bad-mouth when you are absent

Doublethink: The capacity to accept contrary opinions at the same time

Doubling: An insertion with something that results both the vagina and anus being penetrated at a time (Noun)

Doubting Thomas: A person who always doubts

Dropper: The one who passes counterfeit money

Drunkard: A person who is very much drunk

Dry humping: The activity when the two people fully clothed repeatedly keep on rubbing the body on each other especially the genital areas to gain sexual pleasure

DSL: A woman expert in giving blow job to her male partner [Dick sucking lips]

Duff sticking: The activity of a male person when he tries to rub or stick his sexual organ with a standing male or female person in a crowded place

Dullsville: An imaginary place that is extremely dull and boring

Dunce: Someone who is very slow at learning

Duplicity: A person's dishonest behavior in which he is trying to make you believe something which is not true

Dutch sex: The sexual activity of a woman rubbing her breasts with her male partner's genital

Dutch act: Suicide

Dutch auction: A sale of goods in which the price is reduced by the auctioneer until a buyer is found

Dutch cap: A contraceptive cap to prevent pregnancy

Dutch courage: The intoxicating effect of alcohol when a person feels elated and speaks too much

Dutch party: A party in which each person makes a contribution to pay the bill

Dutch uncle: A good advisor of yours who advises you at a needful time

Dynamism: The belief that ultimately the power wins

Dyslexia: A mental problem when a person suffers a severe difficulty in reading and speaking

Dysmenorrhoea: A painful or difficult physical problem caused by menstruation in women

Dysphasia: The lack of coordination in speech owing to brain damage

Dystopia: A place of your imagination in which you think everything is bad

E

Ear-biter: Someone who always tries to borrow money from you

Early bird: A person who gets up early in the morning

Easy cry: Someone who is so emotional that he cries easily

Easy lady: A call-girl or prostitute

Easy money: The money that you earn easily without putting more efforts

Easy-peasy: Very easy

Easyrich: A person who has become easily rich

Easer-ride: A sexually satisfying lover

Easy touch: A person who can be easily exploited financially

Eaves dropper: Someone who listens to others' private talk secretly (Pronounced – eevz dropr)

Eccentric: The man who is odd or unstable in his behavior

Echo chamber: A person who totally agrees with everything another person says

Ecodrums: The financial crisis of a country or the world caused by recession and other problems [Contraction of economical doldrums]

Economic vegetarian: A person who is vegetarian because he can't afford to buy non-vegetarian food

Ecstasy: A feeling of joy when you are extremely happy

Ectopic pregnancy: The pregnancy occurring outside the womb

Eden Garden: A place where you can get every thing and enjoy every moment with great happiness

Edutainment: A subject matter of education combined with entertainment

Effeminate: A man who behaves like a woman

Elbow tag: Your activity when you are sitting in a theater and adjust your posture in such a way that your arm or elbow touches the girl sitting next to you

Electra complex: A mental disorder when a father feels a carnal desire for his own daughter or vice versa

Elocution: The art of clear and expressive speech of distinct pronunciation and articulation

Elopement: The activity of a girl running away with her lover to marry secretly

Eloquent: A person who is able to speak his language properly

Emotional dump: The act of throwing emotional crap onto one or more of your friends

Empathy: The ability to understand other's feeling or experience

Empiricist: Someone who does not believe in any theory, but he works on his own experiment and experience (Pronounced – *im-pirisist*)

Endsville: A place or a situation from where you do not have any further hope

Endurance: The power to tolerate something

Enforcer: A strong-arm man in an underworld gang

Enigma: The thing that is puzzling you

Envious: A positive jealous who wants to compete you without having any bad wishes

Epicenter: The central point of something which is creating difficulty

Epicure: A man with refined taste in food and drink

Episiotomy: The cut made by the doctor on the vagina of a woman when she is going to deliver a child

Equilibrium: A state of mental balance

Erotomania: Excessive sexual desire in a man or woman

Erring sister: A prostitute

Escapist: The man who runs away from truth

Espionage: The activity of secretly getting important political or military information about another country or finding out another company's secrets by using spies

E-thug: An internet thug who takes others' money illegally

Etymology: The source of the formation and development of a word

Eunuch: A human being who is neither male nor female (Pronounced – *yoonak*)

Eunophilia: The practice of having sex with a eunuch [Contraction of eunuch and philia]

Euphoria: An extremely strong feeling of happiness and excitement of false belief

Euphuism: A stylish and attractive way of speaking

Euthanasia: Mercy killing – When a doctor kills a patient who is suffering from an incurable disease

Eve-teasing: An act of teasing a woman with the intention of sexual harassment

Ex: A former husband, wife, or lover

Ex benefits: When a man and woman continue their physical relation even after break up or divorce – that is ex benefits

Ex-con: Ex convict – Someone who has been convicted before

Exegetist: The one who gives critical explanation on religious belief (Pronounced – *eksi-ji-tist*)

Exodus: A situation in which many people leave a place at a time

Exonerate: To free somebody from all blames

Exorcism: The act of a priest or religious person to make an evil sprit leave a place or a person's body

Expatriate: A man who is living in a foreign country

Expiration dating: A date and meeting of the lovers who are soon to get separated

Eye shagging: An act of a man to stare at a woman with the imagination of having sexual gratification

Extempore: Speaking on any topic without preparation

Externee: A criminal who is punished by the court to stay out of his country or a certain place

Extheist: Someone who believed in God before but now he does not believe

Eye tonic: A girl who you often look at while working in an office for some excitement

Extremist: The man whose religious or political opinion is so extreme that he can do any violent of illegal things

Extrovert: A person who likes to spend much time with people

Eye-candy: Something visually arresting but intellectually undemanding

F

F-word: An abusive or bad word starting with the letter 'f'

Face-ache: Someone who looks very sad from his face

Face lift: A medical operation in which the skin of a person's face is tightened

Factotum: An employee who does a wide variety of jobs. Someone who performs troublesome duties for another

Fag: A homosexual male person

Fair minded: Someone who looks at the things and judge it in a fair way

Fair-weather friend: The one who stops being your friend when you are in trouble

Fait accompli: Something that has already happened and you can not change

Faith healing: A method of treating a sick person through the power of belief and prayer

Fall back: A plan or course of action that is ready to be used in an emergency if other things fail

Fallenture: An act of a government when it destroys its own public property but blames the enemy of the country with the intention of starting a war [Contraction of fallen venture]

Fall guy: Someone who is punished for something wrong that somebody else has done, also termed scapegoat

Fall money: The money that a criminal sets aside to use in case he gets arrested

Falsies: The pads that a woman uses to make her breasts look bigger

False dawn: A situation in which you think that something good is going to happen but it does not happen

False flag: The activity of a government or organization to motivate the people to support or fight for an unfair war

Family credit: The monthly payment that the poor people get by the government in some countries

Fanatic: A person who holds extreme and dangerous opinion about his religion

Fancy man: A pimp who arranges customers for a prostitute

Fancy lover: A lover who is not serious in love and that is why he keeps on changing partners

Fancy woman: A man's mistress

Fanny: The female sex organ

Fantabulous: Wonderful

Fantasy: A condition of mind when you are imagining something and you feel that you are in a dream while you are awake

Faraway expression: An expression on your face that shows that your thoughts are far away from your present situation

Far sighted: Someone who can understand the future effect of the action that he is going to take now

Fart king: A man who is strong in speaking but weak in action

Fascism: An extreme political system or attitude which is in favor of strong central government and which does not allow any opposition (Pronounced – *fashizm*)

Fashionably late: The person who prefers reaching late giving an impression to others that he was held up with other work

Fast and furious: A film full of rapid action and sudden changes

Fatalist: Someone who believes that whatever happens in his life is decided by fate and he can not control or change it

Fat chance: A negligible prospect

Faux pas: An action that you take to do something good but something bad happens (Pronounced faw paa)

Feeflow: The vaginal saliva coming out during sexual secretion

Feel-good factor: The hopeful feeling about the future that is shared by many people

Feet of clay: The fault that you can not find out in first sight

Felch: A male homosexual who sucks out the semen of his partner

Fellatio: The sexual activity of sucking or licking a man's sex organ (Pronounced (fa-lei-shio)

Felony: A serious crime such as murder or rape

Feminazi: A woman who supports feminism radically

Feminism: The belief and aim that women should have the same rights and opportunities as men

Fence market: A market of stolen goods

Fender-bender: A person who stages a road accident and pretends that he has been injured so that he can claim compensation

Feng shui: A Chinese system for deciding the right position for a building and for placing objects inside

Fetishist: Someone who believes in some magical power and worships that kind of god

Fever pitch: A very high level of excitement or activity

Fey: A person who is sensitive and rather mysterious and does not act in a very practical way

Fiasco: The work that does not succeed and therefore it embarrasses you

Fickle: A person who is changing his mind in an unreasonable way

Fidelity: The quality of being loyal and faithful to somebody

Fifth column: A group of people living in his own country but working secretly to help the enemy of his country

Figment: Something that somebody has imagined and that does not really exist

Fight of Rhodesia: The fight to overthrow the government of minority community

Finger man: An informer to police

Finger smith: A pickpocket who is expert in stealing money

Finicky: A person who is too much worried about what he eats or wears

Finishing school: A private school where young women from rich families are taught how to behave in fashionable society

First-time stand: First time sex

First world: The rich industrial countries of the world

Fisting: The act of inserting hand into the sexual organ

Five-finger discount: Stealing something from a shop

Flabbergasted: Extremely surprised or shocked

Flagellation: The act of whipping or beating oneself for religious purification

Flak-catcher: An employee to deal with the hostile comments or any offence on the behalf of the person or institution he is working for

Flamboyant: A confident and exciting person who can attract the attention of others

Flasher: The man who shows his sexual organ in public

Flash mob: A large number of people suddenly gathered at a particular place to perform an arbitrary action

Flashpoint: A situation or place in which violence or anger starts

Flattery: The act of praising someone insincerely (Noun)

Flea-bag: A soldier's sleeping bag

Flea market: An outdoor market in which second hand (used) good are sold at low price

Fleetcher: The father or mother who introduces their good-looking daughter to the acquainted persons for some financial benefits

Fellator: A woman who practices oral sex to a man

Flesh trade: Prostitution

Flexisexual: A man who is flexible in his sexual desire and so mostly he is attracted towards girls but sometimes he feels attracted towards boys also

Flighty: A woman who always keeps on changing her ideas, activities and partners without treating them seriously

Flip side: The side part of an idea, argument or action which is not so important

Floating voter: Someone who does not always vote for the same political party and so he has not decided which party he should vote for

Floozy: A woman in sexual relationships with many men

Flunky: A person who tries to please an important and powerful person by doing small jobs in order to gain some favor

Fly-by-night: The man who runs away without paying the money he had borrowed

Fly-flat: A victim of crime

Folk lore: The traditions and stories of a country or community

Fool's paradise: A false happiness that can not last longer

Forbidden fruit: Something that you are not allowed doing therefore it attracts you very much

Foreboding: A strong feeling that something unpleasant or dangerous is going to happen

Foreclosure: The act done of a bank when they take control of somebody's property

Foreplay: A sexual activity of touching and kissing sexual organs

Foresight: The ability to predict what is likely to happen

Forlorn: A lonely and unhappy person

Fortitude: The courage that you show at the time of great pain, difficulties or suffering

Fortune hunter: A man who wants to become rich by marrying a rich woman

Foster father: The man who is taking care of a child as a father

Foundling: A baby who has been abandoned by his parents

Fourth dimension: An experience that is outside normal human experience

Fourth estate: The press media and journalism

Frailty: The weakness in a person's character or morals

Frame of reference: A particular set of ideas, beliefs or experiences that affects how a person understands or judges something

Frame-up: A situation when an innocent person is proven guilty of a crime by producing false evidence

Frantic: Someone who is not able to control his emotion because he is extremely frightened or worried about something

Freebooter: A man who takes part in a war in order to steal goods

Freemasonry: The friendship between the people who have the same profession or interests

French kiss: A kiss with one partner's tongue inserted in the other's mouth

French leave: The leave that you take without informing your senior

French letter: Condom

French sex: Oral sex

Freudian slip: The cleverness of saying something showing it a mistake but in reality you wanted to say that (Pronounced *froidian slip*)

Friday man: An employee who does all kind of work to his boss

Frogfinger: An extremely eccentric man who rapes his daughter

Front passage: The vagina, also termed 'front bottom'

Frozen limit: Something that is going beyond limit therefore you can not tolerate that

Fruition: The successful result of a plan, process or activity

Frump: A woman who wears unfashionable clothes

Fugitive: A person who has escaped and is trying to avoid being caught

Fugly: A very ugly woman

Fundamentalism: The practice of following very strictly the basic rules and teaching of any religion

Funk: Panic

Funkhole: A place to which one can go to avoid danger

Funny bone: The part of the elbow containing a very sensitive nerve that is painful if you hit it

Furor: A great anger or excitement shown by a number of people caused by public events

Furtive: A person who is behaving in a way that shows that he wants to keep something secret and does not want to be noticed

Fusspot: A man who is often worried about unimportant things and is difficult to please

Futuristic: A person or thing which is extremely modern and unusual in appearance as if belonging to future time

G

Gag: The one who is desperately eager for sexual intercourse

Gang-bang: The copulation with an individual by a group

Gangbuster: An officer of a law-enforcement agency in dealing with organized crime

Gatecrasher: A person who comes as an uninvited guest in your party and his intention is to just have food

Generalist: The one who is not a specialist

Generous: A very kind and helpful person

Genocide: The murder of whole race or group of people

Gentleman's: The toilet

Gigolo: The one who takes money from a rich woman to be her lover

Glad eye: An amorous glance

Glad hand: A cordial handshake

Glitch: A sudden brief irregularity or malfunction

Glitz: The glamour of show-business

Glutton: The man who eats too much

Goatee: The hair that is grown on the chin of a male person

Go-getter: The one who is in the way of achieving success

Gongoozler: A person who stares idly at something

Goodish: A person who is trying to look good by wearing good clothes but in fact he is not good

Goody-goody: The one who admires you at your front but speaks all bad things behind

Goofer: Someone who commits mistakes easily

Googler: A person who spends much of his time searching things on Google

Goon: Thug

Goshing gosh: O my god! [An exclamatory expression – 'god' replaced with 'gosh']

Grandiloquent: The one who uses tough words or complicated sentences in speaking or writing to impress people

Grass widow: A woman who has been left by her husband for a long time

Grave crime: A big crime for which death punishment can be given

Graveyard shift: The odd working hour in an office somewhere at late night

Gravy: The unearned or unexpected money

Gravy train: The source of easy unearned financial profit

Gray area: An area of a subject or situation that is not clear or does not fit into a particular group and is therefore difficult to deal with

Greek love: Anal sex

Green horn: An illiterate person

Gregarious: The one who spends a lot of time with friends being least bothered about other things

Grog blossom: The redness of the nose caused by excessive drinking

Grope: To fondle a person's sexual organ or breasts

Grouch bag: A hidden pocket or purse carried in a concealed place for keeping the money safe

Ground zero reality: The bare truth that is not infected with any kind of lies at all

G spot: The part of the female body around front and back of her waist

G string: A thread-like panty worn by women similar to a thong but exposes much more

Guido: A socially unsophisticated person whose behavior is viewed as typically lower class

Gullible: The one who is easily cheated by others because he believes or accepts easily what other people tell him

Gumgoozer: A tactical homosexual man who persuades his male friend in such a way that even the friend hates homosexuality still he makes him agree to for that

Gun moll: An armed woman

Gutter press: The activity of press media, when they publish a lot of shocking news about people's private lives rather than serious news

Grenade: An unattractive girl that you are using to approach a beautiful girl

Gun marriage: The marriage in which the groom is kidnapped and forced to marry

Gynophobia: An abnormal fear from women

H

Hairy eyeball: A look given with narrowed eyes indicating hostility or disapproval

Half-cut: The one who is fairly drunk

Half-humping: An act of sexual intercourse when a man withdraws his penis before ejaculation to prevent pregnancy, also called coitus interruptus

Hallucination: The apparent perception of an object not actually present

Hand-job: An act of masturbation being done by a woman to a man

Hanger-on: The one who tries to be friendly with famous persons In order to get advantage

Hanky-panky: The dishonest dealing

Happy-go-lucky: A person who doesn't care or worry about the future

Hard case: A person aggressively difficult to deal with

Hardhead: An obstinate person

Hard-on: An erection of the penis

Hard liner: The one who follows strict policy or attitude of something

Harem family: A family in which a man has many wives and children and they live together as seen in Arab world

Hatchet man: A hired killer

Headcase: A mentally unstable person

Heart quack: A mental or emotional instability caused by bad incidents

Heavy sugar: A large amount of money

Hedonist: The one who believes pleasure is the most important thing in life

Hell-bent: The one who is determined to do something even though the results may be bad

Head hunter: The one who collects the head of the people they kill

Hellacious: Terrific, awful

Hellmonk: The religious leader involved in extremely illicit activity

Henchman: A faithful supporter of a powerful person

Hen pecked: A man who obeys his wife for everything

Hermit: The one who leads a lonely life for religious reasons

Hibiswig: Swallowing the ejaculated semen during lovemaking

Hieros gamos: An ancient religious ceremony in which the couples gathered in an open place under a tree wearing partly or no clothes and they used to perform sex act chanting and remembering God

High-five: A gesture of celebration or greeting in which two people slap each other's hand with arms extended

High-hat: A snob who thinks he is better than other people because he is more intelligent

Highway man: A man who robs travelers on public roads

Hip-kiss: A kiss placed around the private part of the lover who is fully clothed

Hip-peeping: The considerably earlier erotic feeling in small children

Hirohito's policy: When two parties ask you to solve their problem, but you being a mediator, instead of solving the problem make them fight more for your own benefit – that is Hirohito's policy. (Relating to Japanese commander Hirohito)

Hit list: A list of people to be killed

Hit-man: A hired killer

Hogwash: Nonsense or rubbish talk or writing

Hoity-toity: A person with insincere behavior

Holocaust: A situation in which many things are destroyed and many people are killed

Home-son-in-law: A man who stays at his wife's home

Home body: Someone who doesn't like to go out but enjoys spending time at home

Homesick: Someone who feels very sad because he is away from home and misses his family and friends

Honcho: A leader or boss

Honey-baby: A sweetheart

Honor killing: The act of killing somebody for the sake of the prestige

Hooker: The woman who grows in her career by offering sex to others

Hook-shop: A prostitute's house

Hooligan: A young person who behaves in an extremely noisy and violent way

Hot-air artist: A boaster – The one whose claims or promises sound impressive but have no real meaning or truth

Hot-pants: The erection (noun). *He's got the hot-pants.*

Human trafficking: The crime of selling or forcing people to do bad work after taking them to other countries

Humdinger: An excellent or remarkable person or thing

Hung up: Confused or bewildered

Hunk: A big, strong and attractive man

Hustler: A person who lives by stealing or other means

Hymen: A piece of skin that partly covers the opening of the vagina

Hypocrite: The one who pretends to have a moral standard or opinion but in fact he doesn't have

I

Incest: The sexual crime between a brother and sister or a father and daughter

Indecent assault: A sexual attack on somebody but not rape

Individuality: An outer personality of a person that changes his look different from others

Identikit: The making of a picture with drawings of different features that can be put together to form the face of a person using description given by the witness

Identity crisis: The mental inability when a person does not recognize himself

Idée fixe: An idea that dominates the mind (Pronounced *eedei feex*)

Idiosyncrasy: A person's particular way of behaving or thinking

Iffy: A doubtful person

Illegit: An illegitimate child

Imbo: A gullible person who can be easily cheated

Illusionist: A person who spreads false idea or belief about something

Incarnation: The embodiment of God as a human

Incorrigible: Someone with bad habits which can not be changed

Indie: An independent, theatre, film, or record company

Individuality: An outer personality of a person that changes his look different from others

Inevitable: The thing that you can not avoid or prevent form happening

Inertia: The lack of desire when a person does not want to change himself

Infallible: The one who never makes mistake

Inferiority complex: A feeling that you are not as important or intelligent as other people, opposite to – superiority complex

Infidel: The one who does not believe in his religion

Inginct: An act of a woman when she refuse having sex with her lover just to examine the patience and truthfulness of him. [Contraction of ingenious instinct]

Innovator: Someone who introduces new things or ideas

Inquisitive: The one who is very interested in learning new things and has the curiosity to know different things

Insatiable: The one who can never be satisfied

Inside job: A crime committed by or with the help of someone working in a place where it took place

Inside stand: The placing of a gang member as one of the staff of a place to be robbed, in order to facilitate the robbery

Insolvent: A person who does not have enough money to pay what he has borrowed

Insomnia: The condition of being unable to sleep in night

Instigator: A person who causes something bad to happen

Insular: The one who is interested in his own ideas

Insider: Someone who knows many secrets but he discloses that when right time comes

Intermittent: A woman's second boyfriend who she establishes physical relation with when her first boyfriend is out of station

Internee: The one who has been punished by the court to not go out of a specified place

Introspection: The careful examination of your thoughts, feeling and reasons

Introvert: A quiet person who is more interested in his own thoughts and feeling therefore he doesn't spend time with other people

Insomnia: The condition of being unable to sleep in night

Item: The girlfriend

Itty-bitty: A very small thing

J

Jackpot: A large amount of money that is given to you as a prize in a game

Jackleg: A lawyer or preacher who is incompetent or unscrupulous

Jaffa: An infertile male

Jail bird: A criminal who goes to jail quite often

Jerk off: To masturbate

Jhakas: Something looking very nice

Jhol: A deception

Jilt: A woman who ends a romantic relationship with her lover in a sudden and unkind way

Jingle: Money in small coin

Jinx: A person or thing that brings bad luck

Jobsworth: A day trip, particularly one taken for pleasure and arranged from ones place of work

Johnson brother: A criminal

Jolt: A drink of liquor

Joy house: A brothel

Judgment Day: The day at the end of the world when God will judge everyone

Jugad: A makeshift of something brought to work for a temporary period of time

Juicy kiss: The kiss of a body part after putting sweet liquid on it

Juldy: Haste, hurry

Junkie: A drug addict

K

Kaffir: An unreliable person

Kangaroo court: A court in which the judgment is given in the favor of somebody without investigating the case properly

Keep: A woman who is living with a man without marriage

Key industry: The main industry which the county's economy is depending upon

Kick the bucket: To die (verb)

Kiddo: A kid; used as a familiar form of address to a man or woman

Kidlet: A small child

Kidvid: A television or video program made for children

Killjoy: The one who makes the people upset at the time of enjoyment, also called 'spoil-shot'

Kink: A sexually abnormal person

Kinsman: A far relative of yours from paternal link

Kiss-me-quick: The lock of hair that swings on the face of a woman making her more attractive, also called 'love lock'

Klepto: A thief (The abbreviation of kleptomaniac)

Knee-trembler: An act of sexual intercourse between people standing up

Knockers: A woman's breasts

Knock up: To make a woman pregnant (Verb)

Knocking shop: A place of prostitution

Knockover: Theft (Noun)

L

Lad: A group of male friends

Lady killer: A man who is very famous in women

Lady's man: A man who spends most of his time with women

Lalapaloosa: Something outstandingly good of its kind

Lallygag: Blowjob

Lame excuse: An excuse that can be caught and people can understand that you are telling lies

Lass-lorn: A broken-heart person who is suffering from pain because he is separated from his beloved

Lead: Male sexual potency, vigor (Slang word)

Lecherous: The one who is having strong or excessive sexual desire

Left field: A position away from the center of interest

Left-handed compliment: If somebody is admiring you with the intention of taunting – that is a left-handed compliment

Legal: A passenger who pays the exact fare to a taxi driver without any tip

Legart: Pornography

Lemon-game: Deception

Lesbian: A homosexual woman

Levity: The behavior that shows a lack of respect for something serious

Lexicographer: The one who writes a dictionary

Liaison: A secret sexual relationship

Libertine: A person who leads an immoral life and is interested in pleasure only

Light handed: A very active person who finishes his work fast

Ligger: The one who gatecrashes a party, a gatecrasher

Light skirt: A prostitute

Light hearted: The one who is intended to be amusing or easily enjoyable rather than too serious

Lilting English: The style of speaking English in a very sweet and melodious tone

Limbo: A situation in which you are not certain what you should do next because you are waiting for somebody else to make a decision

Lion hunter: A person who is too eager to develop his contacts with rich and influential people

Lipstick: A lesbian (Slang word)

Logomania: The act of talking too much that can show that the person is mentally ill

Loner: The one who likes to live alone

Loo: The toilet

Looky-frooky: A man who tempts a woman to see pornographic things acting innocently so that he can develop physical intimacy with her

Lorena Bobbitt: A woman who cuts the sexual organ of a man

Loss-leader: The one who sells goods at low price to attract customers

Louisiana loverboy: A married man who in looking for another female partner because he is not happy with his wife

Lounge lizard: A man who frequents fashionable parities in search of wealthy patroness

Love-lorn: A person who has got so much of pain in love

Low-heel: A woman readily agreeing to lie down for sexual intercourse

Lumber: A house where stolen property is hidden

Lunarfall: A perceived fall of white racist America's supremacy after the second time winning of Barack Obama

Lunchbox: The penis being more apparent by tightly fitting trousers (Slang)

Lure-crime: The crime committed in sexual jealousy

Lurking resurrection: The great success that is taking a long time to come, and so, you are facing tremendous problems

Lurkman: A man who lives by stealing money

M

Malarkey: Total nonsense or foolishness

Male dominance: The effect of giving more importance to male than female in a society

Malevolent: The one whose desire is to harm other people

Malinger: The one who pretends to be ill to get rid of his work

Malky: A razor being used as a weapon

Mamma mia: O my god!

Mamzer: The one who is born of a prostitute

Man eater: A woman who is in sexual relationship with many men

March in Moscow: To visit a red-light area for the purpose of seeking enjoyment. In sentence – *Refrain yourself from having a march in Moscow*

Marge: A lesbian who takes the role of the passive or submissive partner

Marriage of convenience: A marriage that is made for practical, financial or political reasons and not for love

Marv: Marvelous, outstanding

Mascot: An animal or toy or anything that people believe will bring them good luck

Masher: A womanizer who makes indecent advances to women in public places

Mash note: A love letter

Masochist: A person who gets pleasure from giving pain to himself or others

Matinee idol: A male actor who is very famous in women

Matriversion: A conversion of someone into another religion for marriage purpose [Blend of matrimonial conversion]

Matriarchy: A system of society led by women

Maverick: A man who does not behave or think like everyone else but he has independent unusual opinions

Maximalist: A person who wants to achieve more and more in his life, opposite to – minimalist

Melancholia: A mental illness when the patient is depressed and worried about unnecessary fears

Mealy mouthed: The one who speaks very less

Mercenary: A man who fights for any group that offers payment

Mental block: The blocked state of mind when he is not able to think anything other than what he normally believes

Mercenary: A man who fights for any group that offers payment

Meritorious: Someone with full of qualities

Metaphysics: The branch of philosophy that deals with the nature of existence, truth and knowledge

Metrosexual: The average heterosexual man who is more concerned to his appearance of a gay man

Mexican shower: When a person does not have bath but wears perfume to hide his body smell

Midlife crisis: The worry, disappointment or lack of confidence that a person may feel in the middle of his life time

Mickey Mouse: Small, insignificant or worthless

Midas touch: Your ability when you can make a lot of money from any work you undertake

Middle leg: The penis

Migrant smuggling: The work of sending people abroad illegally

Midlife slicker: A person of middle age more inclined to mingling with women for developing romantic relationship

Mind-boggling: Mind-blowing

Minerva: The goddess of knowledge and learning

Mirage: An effect of hot air in desert that creates a misapprehension of water

Misanthrope: The one who hates human being

Miscarriage: The process or time of giving birth to a baby before it is fully developed and able to survive

Misery guts: A person who is always gloomy and complaining

Mishap: A small accident or bad luck that does not have serious results

Misogamist: A person who hates marriage

Misogynist: A man who hates women

Misotheist: The one who hates his religion and theological belief

Misper: A missing person

Miss: A miscarriage (Short form)

Missionary position: A posture in sexual activity when a man lies on his female partner

Mitt-reader: A palmist or fortuneteller

Mixed blessing: Something that has both advantages and disadvantages

Mixet: A prostitute called by a married couple to give sexual pleasure to both a husband and wife at a time [Blend of mix it]

Mobster: The head of a mob involved in some bad activity

Mobocracy: The dominance and power of a mob

Modesty: The action of behavior more reserved in terms of attracting attention of the people

Modesty snatcher: A man who outrages the modesty of women

Mokus: The depression caused by loneliness

Moll: The concubine of a criminal

Monkey-man: A weak and servile husband

Monkey parade: A promenade of young men and women in search of bed partners

Monoglot: Someone who speaks or knows only one language

Monopoly: The complete control, possession or use of something

Monotheism: The belief in one god

Morose: A person who looks stupid because of his unhappy and bad tempered behavior

Moon-eyed: Drunk

Moonlight flitting: When a tenant is not able to pay the rent of the place he is living, and so, he runs away in the midnight without paying the rent – that is moonlight flitting

Moonlighter: The man who takes a moonlight flitting

Morning-after pill: A medicine that a woman can take to avoid pregnancy

Morning quarterback: The one who engages in criticism of something

Mortuary: A room in a hospital or some other place where dead bodies are kept

Motorhead: A car or motorcycle enthusiast

Motormouth: The one who has no control on his mouth and so he speaks too much

Morning gift: The gift that a groom gives to his newly wedded wife

Morning sickness: The vomiting sickness during pregnancy

Modesty snatcher: A man who outrages the modesty of women

Moonlight employee: A call girl or prostitute who hides her profession giving excuses of working in a night-shift call center

Monday blues: The tiredness that you feel on Monday after you enjoyed a weekend, and so, you do not want to work

Monomania: A strong concentration of interest upon one particular subject

Mouth honor: The act of giving respect not to the general people but to your own people or who you are familiar with

Mouthpiece: A lawyer (Slang word)

Mr. Big: The head of an organization

Mr. Clean: An honorable or incorruptible politician

Mucker: A vulgar person

Muffin tag: An attempt of a man to sit closed to a female traveler to feel the touch of her body

Multifarious: A person with lots of talents

Multivocal: The one who knows or speaks many languages

Munchausen's syndrome: The mental abnormality when a person pretends or tries to show that he is sick so that the people should pity him

Mummery: The meaningless festival or ceremony

Muff-diver: A man who practices cunnilingus

Mug shot: A photograph of a person in police records

Mumping: The acceptance by the police of small gifts or bribes from the trade-people

Munjon: An Australian Aborigine who has a little experience of white society and its customs

Mummery: The meaningless festival or ceremony

Murphy's Law: The supposed tendency of things to go wrong in a perverse or annoying way, also called 'Sod's law'

Myopic: The one who is not able to think outside his own situation

Mystery: A young and inexperienced girl to a city-life (Slang word)

Mythiciser: A person who creates false stories to make the people believe in religious incidents

N

Nab: To arrest someone in wrongdoing

Nasty: A traumatic experience or concealed unpleasantness in a person's background

Natural call: The feel to go to toilet

Narcissism: The habit of admiring oneself too much

Neatnik: The one who is neat in his or her personal habits

Necrophagous: The one who eats the flesh of dead body

Necromancy: The practice of claiming to communicate with the dead by magic in order to learn about the future

Necrophilia: A kind of madness when a person wants to have sex with a dead body

Needle: A fit of irritation (Slang word)

Needle man: The man who injects himself with drugs

Nepotist: Someone who give unfair benefits to his own family when he is in a position of power

Neophyte: A person who is newly converted into a religion

Nerd: A foolish

Net-head: A person obsessed with using the internet

Newbie: A person new to some activity

New world: North and South America

Niagara shower: A woman's first sexual intercourse (Relating to *Niagara fall* in America)

Nig: A black person

Niggergram: A rumor or piece of gossip

Nilor: A man having no girlfriend

Nightmare: An experience that is very frightening and unpleasant or very difficult to deal with

Nine-days wonder: A short period of happiness

Nitty-gritty: The reality or practical details of a matter

Nob: A person of wealth or high social position

Nobbins: The coins collected by a performer after an entertainment

Nocturnal emission: A dream full of sexual excitement in which a man ejaculates, also called wet-dream

Nodding funk: A situation full of confusions and disturbance when a man is not sure whether his female companion would allow him to have sex with her. In sentence – *I am in a nodding funk.*

Non-denominational: The one who is not restricted to any religion

No-hoper: A useless or incompetent person

Nonce: A sexually mad person

Nooner: A daytime sex

Nork: An act of licking breasts in lovemaking

Nosy parker: A person who is too much interested in other people's affair

Nonage: The ancient time when human mind was not developed

Nostalgia: A feeling of sadness, which is mixed with pleasure and affection when you think of happy times in the past

Notell: A motel used for illicit sexual assignations

Notorious: A person with bad fame and popularity

Novice: A person who is new and has a little experience in a skill, job or situation

Numskull: A fool

Nuptial tie: The bondage of marriage

Nutcase: An eccentric or lunatic person

Nymphomania: Excessive sexual desire in women

O

Object soul: Someone who objects everything

Obscupant: The one who objects social development

Obsolete: A thing that is no longer in use because something new has been invented

Oculist: Someone who practices black magic

Odalisque: A female slave kept by a rich man for sexual pleasure

Oedipus complex: An abnormality when a man starts feeling sexual desire for his mother or the mother feels the same for her son

Officious: The one who is too ready to tell the people what to do

Off money: Bribe

Ombudsman: A mediator between two parties to solve a dispute

Omega trap: The sharp practice of a prostitute pretending to be your beloved

Omniscient: The one who knows everything

One finger salute: To show the middle finger of the hand to someone as a matter of disgust

One-night stand: A sexual relationship of one night

One-way pockets: The pockets of a miser person

Onion: A woman with whom several men have intercourse one after another (Slang word)

Oomph: Sex appeal

Open faced: The person whose thought can be easily understood by seeing his face

Operation false flag: The activity of a government or organization to motivate the people to support or fight for an unfair war

Oppressor: A man who treats somebody in a cruel and unfair way

Organ: The penis

Orphan paper: A bad cheque

Ort: The anus

Out spoken: Someone who says exactly what he thinks, even if it shocks or offends people

Out law: A person who has done something illegal and is hiding to avoid being caught

Overhung: The one who is suffering from a hang-over

Overjolt: The overdose of a drug

P

Pacifist: The one who believes in peace and refuses to fight in war

Paganism: The religious belief which is not the part of any of the world's main religions

Panacea: Something that will solve all the problems of a particular situation (Pronounced *panaasia*)

Pandora box: The one problem, that is so sensitive and dangerous that if you go to solve it, it will open so many other problems

Panhandler: A street beggar

Pantheism: The belief in many or all gods or believing that God is present in all natural things

Pantsing: The action of pulling down someone's trousers or underpants as a practical joke

Paper hanger: The one who passes forged or fraudulent cheques

Paper horse: A person or a team who fails to accomplish a certain task of your expectation

Paparazzi: A photographer who follows famous people around in order to get interesting photos

Paramour: A lover of a married woman

Parlor-house: An expensive type of brothel

Parole: A permission that is given to a prisoner to leave prison before the end of his sentence on the condition that he behaves well

Passive debt: The money that you had given to somebody as a loan but you can not get it back

Paternalist: The person who obeys their parents

Paternity suit: A court case intended to prove who the father of a child is

Payola: A bribe or other secret payment to induce someone to use his or her influence for promoting a commercial product

Peanut: Someone small or unimportant

Peck's bad boy: A wild, unmanageable, or mischievous boy

Pedant: Someone who is proud of his knowledge or learning

Pederast: A man too much inclined to have sex with small children

Pedophilia: The abnormality of having sex with small children

Pee-peeping: The abnormal activity of a man intending to see a woman using toilet

Pegging: The act of sexual activity when a woman uses strap-on dildo to penetrate into her male partner

Penman: A forger (Slang)

Pep talk: False courageous talk

Perjury: The crime of telling a lie in the court of law after you have sworn to tell the truth

Persecution complex: A type of mental illness in which one feels that the other people are trying to harm him

Permissive: A person who shows a free behavior in sexual matter

Pervert: A person with abnormal sexual behavior in which he or she may be interested in animal-sex or some other strange activities

Pervics: A person who gets bore from things easily

Pessimist: The one who always expects bad things to happen

Petticoat government: The dominance of a wife on her husband

Philanthrope: The one who loves mankind

Philistine: A person who hates his culture or art

Philology: The scientific study of the development of a language

Philogynist: A man who likes women very much

Phonology: The study of speech sound and pronunciation of a language

Picasso: A desperate and restless person who is trying to learn something with unstable mind

Pig parliament: The blind, careless and cunning government of a country which is not willing to do anything for the betterment of the people

Pimp: The person who arranges customers for a prostitute

Pink chamber: A good looking female staff appointed in an office to keep all the male staffs energized

Pink prescription: The immoral and illegal practice of a doctor when he gives the wrong information about a disease intending to earn more money from you

Pipecam: A criminal act of a person when he captures the nude video of someone's private life to sell it online (Noun)

Pip-pip: Good bye

Pirate: To form a casual friendship with someone with a view to sexual intercourse

Pisher: Someone who urinates in bed while sleeping

Pissing contest: A futile or purposeless contest

Piss-up: A complete mess-up

Pixilated: A person who is mildly insane

Pizzazz: Vitality or zest

Placebo: The substance which looks like a medicine, is given to a patient who does not need medicine and so the substance has no physical effect

Placer: Someone who deals in stolen goods

Plagiarist: The one who copies another person's ideas or work

Platonic love: The love with no involvement of sex

Play boy: A rich man who spends his time enjoying himself

Pledgitive: A person who abandons their pledged religious life and joins worldly life [Contraction of pledge fugitive]

Pleonasm: The use of more words than needed in language

Plonk: A female police officer

Pluperfect: (An adjective used as an intensifier) – *What the pluperfect have you got to do?*

Plutocracy: A government by the richest people of the country

Plutomania: The desire to earn excessively more and more money

Plutish: A person involved in plutocracy

Pocket billiards: The act of masturbation keeping the hand in trouser pocket (Noun)

Pocketbook: The vagina (Slang)

Poena: An exercise given as punishment to a child

Poindexter: An over-industrious student

Pointy-head: An intellectual

Poker-faced: The one having a humorless expression

Politricks: Politics regarded as being characterized by dishonesty or self-interest [Blend of politics and trick]

Polygamy: The custom of having more than one wife at a time

Polyglot: The one who knows many languages

Polyandry: The custom of having more than one husband at a time

Polytheism: The belief in many gods

Pom-pom: Sexual intercourse

Ponce: A man who lives off prostitute's earning

Poodle-faker: A man who cultivates a female group or society for personal advancement

Poopsy: A sweetheart or girlfriend

Poopy suit: A one-piece garment providing protection for the whole body

Pork barrel: The funds obtained by political influence

Porn picrix: A person who edits a normal photo to look like nude and sells online illegally

Portuguese parliament: A noisy discussion when everybody talks and nobody listens

Position 69: A posture in sexual activity in which a man and woman can lick each other's sexual organ at a time

Position 99: Anal sex

Position fireturn: A posture when a woman positions her body in such a way that the man can have vaginal and anal intercourse with her at a time

Postal: To behave violently as a result of stress. In sentence – *Stop going postal like this.*

Postilion: The anal stimulation of a partner with the finger

Posthumous: A child who is born after his father's death (Pronounced – *postyumas*)

Post-traumatic stress disorder: A medical condition in which a person suffers mental and emotional problem resulting from an experience that shocked him very much

Pot companion: The person who accompanies you at the time of drinking alcohol

Pot belly: A person with big stomach

Pot-smoker: A marijuana smoker

Power monger: Someone with the greed of acquiring power

Prankster: A person who creates troubles for others and enjoys doing that

Prejudice: An unreasonable dislike or preference of a person, group or custom when it is based on their race or religion

Presentiment: A feeling that something unpleasant is going to happen

Prick-teaser: The woman who attracts her lover but finally refuses to get along physically. Also called 'vagina drop'

Private: The genital

Probation: 1.A time of training and testing when you start a new job to see if you are suitable for the work. 2. A system in law that allows a person who has committed a crime not to go to jail if he behaves well and if he meets an official regularly for a fixed period of time

Profanity: Speaking abusive or insulting words

Prop doctor: The doctor who misguides their patients to earn more money

Propeller: Someone with an obsessive interest in computers or other technology

Protocol: A system of fixed rules and formal behavior used at official meetings

Provincialism: The attitude of the people when they are not concerned to the entire country but their own province only

Psyche: The mind, or your deepest feeling and attitude (Pronounced – *saiki*)

Psychodrama: A way of treating mentally ill people by encouraging them to act events from their past to help them understand their feelings

Psychopath: A person suffering from serious mental illness that causes him to behave in a violent way

Pubic hair: The hair near the sexual organs, also called 'pubes'

Pubic symphysis: The surrounding area of a woman's vagina full of sexual sensitivity

Pudendum: Vagina

Pull a job: To commit a robbery (Verb)

Pump metal: To shoot bullets (Verb)

Punk-ass: A good-for-nothing person

Purler: Something excellent or outstanding

Purse proud: The one who is proud of his wealth

Push money: The commission on sold items

Putty medal: An appropriately worthless reward for insignificant service

Pyromania: An obsessive desire to set fire to things

Q

Queer bashing: the rape of a homosexual

Queer Street: Difficulty or trouble. In sentence – *I am in Queer Street*

Quickie: A sexual act of very short time

Quiv: A girl who is more willing to have physical relation with her boyfriend in first meeting

Quandong: Someone who looks after his or her own interest disreputably

Quim: The vulva

R

Race suicide: When a married couple decides to not give birth to any child in order to control the population of the country – that is race suicide

Racism: The unfair treatment of people who belong to a different race

Radicalist: A person who favors complete political or social change and for that he can do anything that can harm people

Rain maker: A highly successful person

Rampsman: Someone who commits robbery with violence

Ramrod: An erect penis

Rapture: A feeling of extreme pleasure and happiness

Rat pack: A disorderly mob of youths

Raunchy: A person who is very naughty in sexual activity

Rave party: A rapturous and illicit party with loud music and dance

Raver: Someone who is passionately enthusiastic about a particular thing

Razor mouth: A person who does not let other people talk because he cuts them short before they complete saying

Razzle-dazzle: The excitement or noisy publicity

Reactionary: Someone who does not like his social setup

Realist: A person, who sees, accepts and deals with the situations as they are real, and so, he is not influenced by his emotion or false hopes

Recluse: Someone who lives alone for religious reason

Recidivist: The one who continues to commit crime and seems unable to stop even after being punished

Red-light area: A part of town for prostitution

Red rampage: The act of having sex with a woman who is having menstruation

Red tape: The official rules that is more complicated than necessary and prevent things from being done quickly

Renaissance man: A person who develops new interest in a particular subject or art

Renegade: The one who opposes and lives outside of a group that he used to belong to

Rental-behind: A male homosexual prostitute

Resilient: The one who is able to feel better quickly after something unpleasant of shocking thing has happened in his life

Resurrection: A new beginning of something

Retard: A mentally retarded person

Reverse manipulation: The act when you make somebody so anxious that he will do the work that will benefit you

Rib-joint: A brothel

Rimming: The sexual act of licking the anus of a partner, also called 'anilingus'

Ring leader: The leader of a criminal group

Rise: An erection of the penis

Rivol: Your husband's another wife is your rivol

Roach: A cockroach

Road hog: An inconsiderate driver or cyclist

Roller: A thief who robs drunken people. A prostitute who steals from her clients

Rolling stone: The one who keeps on changing his job, opinion or ideas

Rotten apple: A man who is very dangerous and harmful to the group he is in because he misguides other

Rough diamond: The one who has many good qualities but he does not look polite and educated

Rough spin: A misfortune or piece of bad luck

Rough tongued: A person with bad manner of speaking

Rough trade: The homosexual prostitution

Rubber: A condom, also called 'French letter'

Rubicon: A point at which you can not change the decision that you have already taken or you can not step back also

Ruckus: A commotion or disturbance

S

Sack rat: A person who spends too much time in bed

Sacrilegious: The one who treats a holy thing or place without respect

Sadistic: The person who gets pleasure from hurting other people

Salad days: The time when you are young and enjoy a lot because neither you have any worry nor any experience

Salvation: The state of being saved from the power of evil

Saltash luck: A miserable task that involves getting wet while doing

Sanitary napkin: A tampon – The thick piece of soft material that women wear outside their body to absorb the blood during the period

Satanism: The system of worshiping a Satan or devil

Satellite: A person who tries to be friendly with a famous person in order to get some advantage

Saturday-night secretary: A female secretary who is working in a company keeping a romantic relationship with her boss

Scamster: The one who is very clever and dishonest in planning of making money

Scandalous: A person who gets involved in a bad or immoral activity to be famous

Scapegoat: A person who is blamed for something bad that somebody else has done

Scaramouch: A coward man who admires himself a lot

Scarlet woman: A woman who is in relationship with many men

Scatterbrain: The one who forgets things and cannot think in organized way

Schizophrenia: A mental illness when a person is unable to link his thoughts, emotion and behavior that makes him unstable with reality and personal relationship (Pronounced – *skitsofreenia*)

Schiz: A person suffering from schizophrenia

Schlimazel: A person who is consistently unlucky. (Pronounced – *shlimozl*)

Scorcher: A very hot day

Screenager: A young person who is at ease using computer technology with new media features

Scumbag: A condom

Scuzzy: Someone disgusting in appearance

Secko: A sexual pervert

Second banana: A supporting comedian

Second god: Money

Seducer: A man or woman who persuades somebody for sex

Segregation: The policy of separating people of different races and religions

Self pleaser: A selfish person

Self pollute: To masturbate (verb)

Separatist: A member of a group of people within a country who want to separate from rest of the country

Seventh heaven: A state joyfulness. In sentence – *My friend is in seventh heaven.*

Sexational: A thing which is sexually sensational

Sexilent: A very sexy woman

Sexpert: An expert who gives advices on sexual matter

Shake-down: A forced contribution

Shambolic: Something which is extremely disorganized (Adjective)

Sharp practice: The act of cheating somebody

Sharpie: A person with extremely provocative style of dress and hair

Shellback: A person of long experience and reactionary views

She-male: A passive male homosexual

Shirker: A person who puts off his work

Shonk: Someone engaged in illegal business activities

Shoo-fly: A policeman in plain clothes whose job is to watch and report on other police officers

Shop lifting: Stealing goods from a shop

Short-arm: An inspection of the penis for sexual disease or other infection (Noun)

Short time: A brief stay in a hotel for sexual purposes

Shotgun marriage: The marriage that takes place quickly because the bride is already pregnant

Shunt: A road accident

Shutter-bug: An enthusiastic photographer

Siamese: The one of the two people who is born with their body joined in some way or sharing the same organs

Sickstick: A mild pervert man who enjoys penetrating his anus with sticks

Signora: Madam

Signora Effect: The tiredness or weakness caused after having too much of sex

Silly billy: A foolish or feeble minded person

Silent majority: The large numbers of people in a country who think the same but don't express their views publically

Silent tower: A place where dead human bodies are kept for religious reasons

Silver spoon: Prosperity or richness

Silver tongue: The one who praises others dishonestly or talks sweetly to get some benefits

Sin city: A city of recklessness and vice

Sitter: Someone employed to sit in a bar and encourage other patrons to buy drinks

Size zero: The look of a slim woman

Slanderer: A person who gives a malicious, false, and injurious statement about another

Skell: A homeless person who sleeps in a subway

Skid row: A part of town frequented by vagrants and alcoholic people

Skin-flick: An explicitly pornographic film

Skin house: An illegal theatre showing pornographic films

Skint: A person without any money left

Skirt chaser: A male person who keeps on looking for new girls to go to bed with

Skirt patrol: A search for female sexual partners

Skull-buster: Very challenging problem

Slacker: An aimless young person with lack of ambition

Slanderer: A person who gives a malicious, false, and injurious statement about another

Slaphead: A bald person

Sledging: An attempt by the fielders to upset a batsman's concentration

Sleeping dictionary: A foreign woman with whom a man has a sexual relationship and from whom he learns some words of her language

Slicker: A smart of sophisticated person

Slips between hand and mouth: The difficulties someone is facing in earning his living. In sentence – *He is facing a lot of slips between hand and mouth.*

Slip-point flickering: The activity of a man looking at a girl in an office without her notice

Slit: The vulva (Slang)

Sloane Ranger: A fashionable and conventional upper-middle-class young person

Slob: A lazy, dirty and untidy person

Slush fund: A reserve fund used for political bribery

Smart mouth: A person who is good at giving retort

Smasher: A sexually attractive man or woman

Smasheroo: A great success

Smoke-up: An official notice that a student's work is not up to the required standard

Snafu: An utter confusion or chaos

Snarf: To eat or drink quickly or greedily (Verb)

Snifty: Haughty or disdainful

Snit: A state of agitation

Snollygoster: An unprincipled person in politics or other group

Snobby: If you think you are better than other people because you are more intelligent, and so, you give importance to high social class, you will be called snobby

SnM: Sadomasochism – The enjoyment from hurting somebody and being hurt in sexual activity

Snooper: Detective

Sob sister: A female journalist who writes sentimental articles. An actress who plays sentimental roles

Soco: A police officer trained to examine senses of crime for forensic evidence

Sodawater effort: An effort which ends before bringing any result

Sodophilia: An abnormal inclination for anal sex

Sodomission: A permission that a man asks from his female partner to go for anal sex
Soft soap: Flattery

Soft touch: A person who can be easily manipulated

Soldier's farewell: An abusive farewell

Soliloquy: A speech in a play when a character speaks his thoughts aloud alone on the stage

Soliloquent: A person who talks to himself

Solitude: The state of being alone that makes you feel happy

Sometimey: An unstable person

Songs smith: The one who writes a song

Sophist: The one who is very clever in speaking or able to understand difficult or complicated ideas

Sourpuss: A miserable person

Souvenir: A thing that you buy to remind you a place or an occasion

Spacy: Someone in the state of euphoria or disorientation (Adjective)

Sparrow brain: A person with limited intelligence

Sparrow cop: A police who is assigned low-grade duties such as patrolling parks

Speak easy: An illegal alcohol shop

Spear-carrier: An actor with a walk-on part. An unimportant participant

Spec: A commercial speculation of future success or gain (Noun)

Spinster: A woman who is getting older but not willing to marry

Splendiferous: Magnificent

Split personality: The mental disorder when a person gets a fit of anger that makes him forget himself and he starts behaving in a very violent way

Spod: An obsessively studious person

Sophist: The one who is very clever in speaking or able to understand difficult or complicated ideas

Sponger: The one who gets money and food from other people without doing anything

Spoil-shot: A person who makes you suddenly sad while you are enjoying

Squarehead: Someone with no criminal convictions

Squaresville: A conventional place or institution, also called 'cubesville'

Squeaky clean: Something above criticism (Adjective)

Squillionaire: A multi-millionaire

Stable: A prostitute permanently fixed for a man or organization (Slang)

Stalwart: The one who can do lot of work for an organization

Star prisoner: The one who is gone to jail for the first time

Starvation: The state of suffering or dying of no food

Steaming: The action of a gang rushing through a public place robbing bystanders or passengers by force of numbers

Stem-winder: A forceful energetic person

Sticky wicket: A difficult situation

Sting operation: A clever secret plan by the media persons to catch criminals

Stoic: The one who is able to suffer pain or trouble without complaining

Straight: The one who is not homosexual

Strap-hanger: A standing passenger in a bus

Strip tease: A form of entertainment in a bar or club, when a performer removes his or her clothes in sexually exciting way in front of an audience

Stud: A man of great sexual prowess

Subdeb: A girl who will soon come out as a debutante

Substitute: A woman's second boyfriend who she establishes physical relation with when her first boyfriend is out of station, also called 'intermittent'

Sugar daddy: A rich older man who flirts with much younger woman

Supergrass: A criminal who informs the police about the activity or other criminals for less punishment

Sunset trip: A trip of roaming around with your lover especially in the evening after getting out of office

Surrogate mom: A woman who gives birth to a baby for another woman who is unable to conceive

Suspended sentence: A punishment given to a criminal in a court of law which means that he will only go to prison if he commits another crime within a particular period of time

Suspended animation: A feeling that you cannot do anything because you are waiting for something to happen

Suspended hooker: A prostitute who posts her profile on matrimonial websites to attract clients

Swallow: A woman employed in an intelligence service to seduce men for the purpose of espionage

Swifty: The one who thinks and acts quickly

Swindle sheet: A document of an account containing fraudulent claims

Swinger: The one who engages in group sex or partner-swapping

Swiss itch: A method of drinking spirits licking salt and lemon

Switcheroo: A surprising change or unexpected twist in a story (Pronounced — swicharoo)

Switch-hitter: A bisexual person

Sycophant: A servile flatterer

Sysop: A system operator assisting in the running of computer network

T

Tampon: A piece of cotton material that a woman puts inside her innerwear to absorb blood during her period

Table-ender: An act of copulation on a table

Tafia: Any supposed network of prominent or influential people which is strongly nationalistic

Tailgate: To drive too close behind another vehicle (Verb)

Talent spotter: The one who looks for new talented persons

Tarzan: A well-built, broad-chest and tall man

Tea room: A public lavatory used for homosexual act by gay people (Slang)

Technoterate: A technically literate person with good knowledge of technology

Tedonist: The people who believe that filling stomach and fulfilling sexual desire is the only purpose of human life on earth [Resembling to hedonist]

Teeny-bopper: A young teenager who follows the latest fashion in clothes and music

Teetotaler: The one who doesn't drink wine or take any narcotic things

Teleology: If you think there is a purpose behind whatever is happening in the world – this thinking is called teleology

Telepathy: The direct communication of thoughts or feelings from one person to another without using speech, writing, or any other method

Tender hearted: A person with a very soft heart

Tenderloin: A district of a city where vice and corruption are common

Tender feeling: Love

The hereafter: The world after death

The Maker: God

Theist: The one who believes in the existence of God

Theocracy: The government of a country by religious leaders

Theodiversity: The diversity or the conflicts between two religions or their belief

Theorist: The one who develops ideas and principles about a particular subject in order to explain why things happen or exist

Thought reader: The one who is so expert that he knows what other people are thinking

Thousand-miler: A dark shirt of yours which you do not wash regularly because it does not show the dirt

Threesome: A sexual act with the involvement of three persons, also called 'troilism'

Time pleaser: Opportunist

Tinseltown: Hollywood

Tiswas: A state of nervous agitation or confusion (Pronounced – tiswoz)

Third degree: The act of threats or violence to get information from somebody

Thunderbox: A toilet

Time pleaser: Opportunist

Titty wank: The act of a female, when she rubs her nipples in the sexually sensitive area of a man to stimulate him for sex

Tochan: The unnecessary lecture or instructions

Toddler: A child who is learning to walk

Tomboy: A young girl who behaves like a boy

Tomcat: To pursue women for the sake of sexual gratification (Verb)

Torch: To set fire in order to claim insurance money

Torpedo: An armed criminal

Tosser: A female erotic dancer

Touch-me-not: The one who does not like to mingle with people and keeps himself reserved

Toy boy: A male lover or husband who is younger than his beloved or wife

Traditionalist: A strong follower of tradition

Transsexual: The one who behaves like a member of opposite sex or who wants to change his sex

Trickster: Cheater

Troilism: A sexual activity involving three people

Trojan horse: A person or thing that is used to deceive an enemy in order to achieve a secret purpose

Trollies: Women's underpants

Trouble and strife: Wife

Trum: The penis of considerably large size [Derivation of tumescent]

Tuft hunter: A person who is eager to make contacts with rich and powerful people

Turf war: The fight among criminals over the right to operate an area

Tumescent: A man with large sexual organ

Turn coat: The one who changes his political party or religious group very frequently

Twirltag: To remarry ones ex wife or husband. (Verb – *Do you think you should twirltag this year*)

Twist: A woman (Slang)

Two-pot screamer: Someone who becomes easily drunk

U

Uglies: Depression (Slang)

Under employment: The situation when the people are not getting the job that can make full use of their skills and abilities so they start doing the jobs of lower standard

Under-handed: Fraud

Undersexed: A person with weak sexual power

Upper story: The human head (Slang)

Upstart: A newly rich person

Usurer: The one who lends money to people at unfairly high rates of interests (Pronounced yoozarər)

Utopia: An imaginary place or state in which everything is perfect

U tuber: Someone who searches for explicit videos on U Tube or internet

U turn: The time when you completely change your policy which was not expected by the people

U wear: Underwear

Uxorious: The one who loves his wife very much

V

Vagabond: A person who has no homes so he travels from place to place

Vaginoplasty: A reconstructive surgery procedure used to construct or reconstruct vaginal canal and mucous membrane

Vainglorious: A man who is too proud of his abilities or achievements

Vampire: A dead person who leaves his or her grave at night to suck the blood of living people

Vandalism: The crime of destroying or damaging public property deliberately

Vanguard: The leaders of a movement in a society

V-drop: Vagina drop – The activity of a woman to attract her lover but refuse to have physical relation at the time of sexual excitement

Venereal disease: Relating to sexual disease

Venus: The goddess of sex

Versatile: Someone who is able to do many things

Vibrator: An electronic device to be used by women for sexual pleasure

Vidiot: A habitual and obsessed watcher of television or player of video games

Virginity: The state of a person who has never had sex

Virginia jaundice: A common but persistent thinking of some men to get married with virgin girls only

Virility: The sexual power in men

Voluptuous: A woman with large breasts and hip

Voracious: The one who eats too much

Voyeur: The one who gets pleasure by secretly watching other people having sex

W

Wag: A female partner of a male celebrity

Wallflower: A neglected or socially awkward person

Wanderlust: Someone who keeps travelling from places to places

Wanker: A masturbator man

Warez: The illegal copies of commercial software and its distribution (Pronounced weərz)

Warm hearted: An enthusiastic and courageous person

Watering cabin: A place where alcoholic refreshment is available

Weak bladder: The one who urinates frequently

Well-hung: A man with a large genital

Wetback: The one who enters the US illegally

Wet blanket: 1 A friend of yours who has stopped talking to you. 2 The one who is not enthusiastic about anything

Wetcourse: Sexual act during bath

Wet dream: A dream full of sexual excitement that leads to ejaculation

Wetleg: A self-pitying person

White ant: A person who fails in their sanity or intelligence, a synonym of 'pledgitive'

White-collar job: An officer-class job that you do sitting in an office

White elephant: A thing that it is useless and no longer needed for you because you spend a lot of money in order to maintain it

White flagger: A person who easily accepts defeat and stops fighting

White hope: The hope that you think cannot bring success

White knight: A company that comes to the aid of another facing an unwelcome take-over bid

White lie: The lie that people can understand easily

White night: The night that you passed without sleeping or could not sleep

White slave: A woman who is forced to become a prostitute

Whizz-boy: A pickpocket

Whorer: A man who goes to a prostitute quite often

Wife swapping: The act of exchanging wife with someone else's in a party or club

Wisdom tooth: Any of the four large teeth at the back of the mouth that do not grow until you are an adult

Windbag: A person who talks a lot but says little of value

Winkler: The one who assists in the eviction of tenants

Wiseacre: The one who shows that he is wise but in fact he is not

Womanizer: A man who persuades women

Woofits: A feeling that you are unwell which is just in your head

Workaholic: A person who works very hard

Working girl: A prostitute (Slang)

Worldly minded: The one who has a lot of experience and knows how he should live in the world

Wowser: An extremely prudish person

Wrongside injector: A doctor with a weak caliber who gets sensual while treating female patients

X

Xenophobe: The one who hates foreigners

X rated: A film or something that people under 18 are not allowed to see

X factor: If you have some special quality than usual for a purpose – that is X factor

X-rayser: A sexually obsessed man who looks at women with piercing eyes

Y

Yardie: An African man engaged in drug-related organized crime

Yellow-belly: A coward

Yellow peril: A strong mindset of a person when he feels that without following the western culture the other countries cannot progress

Yellow journalism: The activity of press media making the news sensational to attract viewers

Yenta: A nagging woman

Yo-yo English: The bad and corrupt English being used by some Africans and other nationals

Z

Zigzig: Sexual intercourse (Slang)

Zillion: A very large number

Zillionaire: A very rich person

Zionist: The racist and fascist white American

Zipdown: Sexual intercourse

Zipless: A person very passionate about sexual encounter

Zoanthropy: The madness when a person starts feeling that he is an animal

Zombie: The one who seems only partly alive without any feeling or interest in what is happening

To get fancy words of English, please refer to my book titled 'English Dictionary of Modern Slang'

Niranjan Jha
Email: cromosys@yahoo.com
www.cromosys.in
www.facebook.com/cromosys
+91-9561450045

"Reading is the sublime engagement of people with optimism."

NIRANJAN JHA SHOWMAN

Founder - Niranjan Jha Showman

Education and Technology Research Center

Patankar Park, Nallasopara (W), Mumbai. +91-9561450045

Education, Technology, Publication, Healthcare, Newsmedia, Realtor, Filmmaking

www.facebook.com/cromosys

Cromosys Publication

Teach
Yourself
German

NIRANJAN JHA SHOWMAN

Cromosys Publication
Teach Yourself French
NIRANJAN JHA SHOWMAN

Cromosys Publication
Teach
Yourself
Spanish
NIRANJAN JHA SHOWMAN

Cromosys Publication

English
Voice
Accent and
Pronunciation

NIRANJAN JHA SHOWMAN

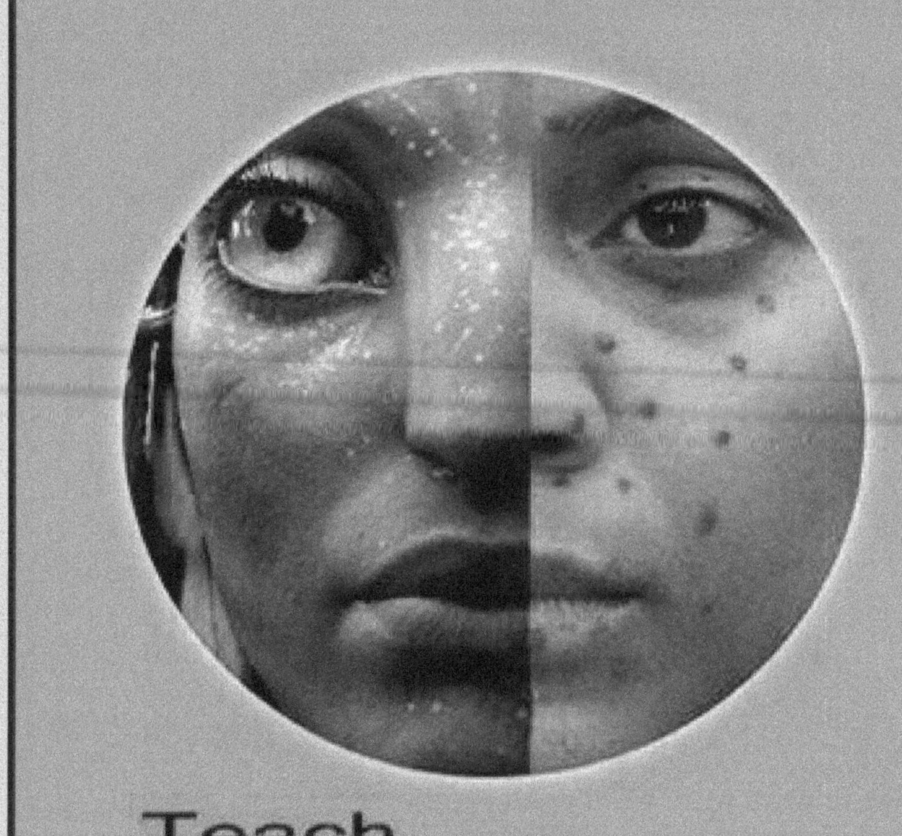
Teach
Yourself
Autodesk
MAYA
Cromosys Publication
NIRANJAN JHA SHOWMAN

Cromosys Publication
Teach
Yourself
Autodesk
3ds Max
NIRANJAN JHA SHOWMAN

Cromosys Publication
CRIMINAL FACTORY
NIRANJAN JHA SHOWMAN

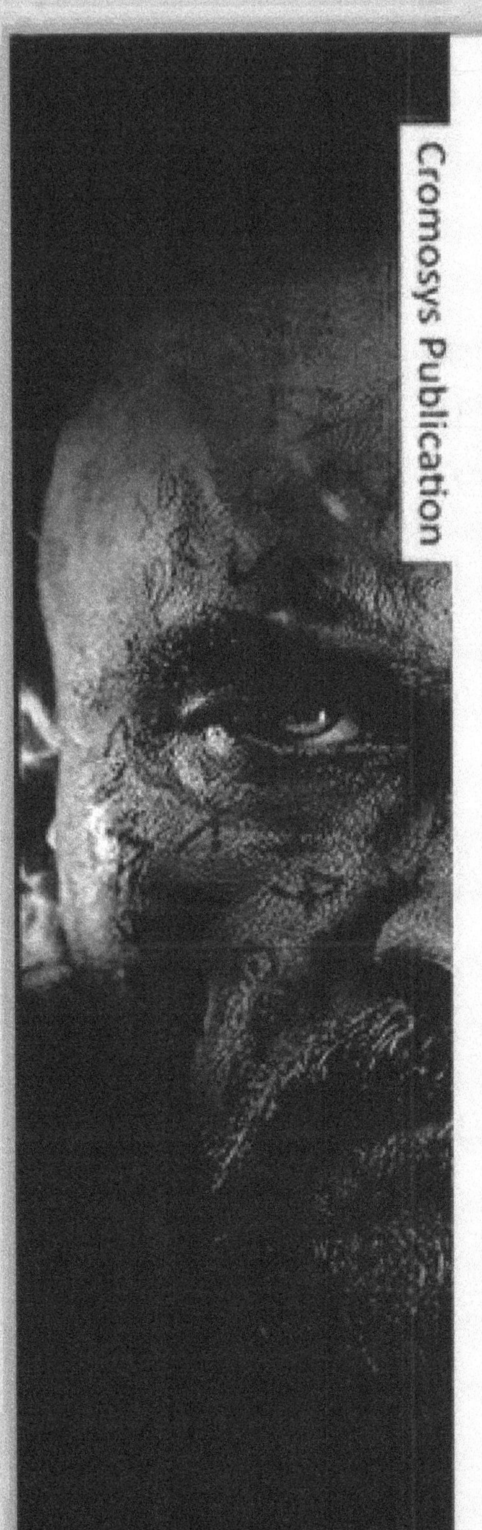

Cromosys Publication
FOCAL DISASTER
NIRANJAN JHA SHOWMAN

Cromosys Publication
Your talents will not help you succeed without your skill of using them.
NIRANJAN JHA SHOWMAN
BE
MILLIONAIRE
LIKE
ME

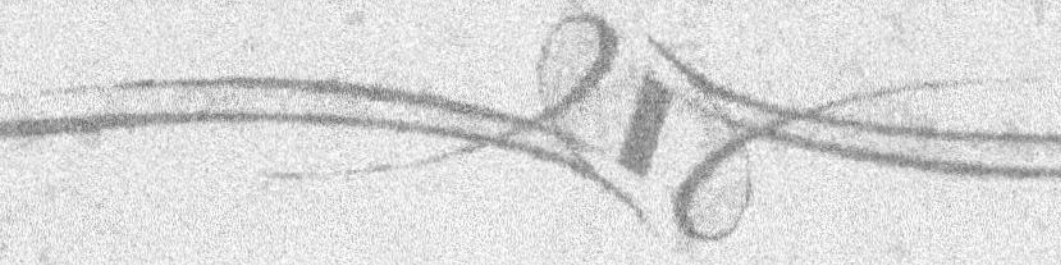

Copyright Office
Government of India

सत्यमेव जयते

Extracts
from the Register
of Copyrights

1.	Registration Number	:	**L-76868/2020**
2.	Name, address and nationality of the applicant	:	NIRANJAN JHA SHOWMAN, CROMOSYS PUBLICATION, 001, JAYSATYAM, PATANKAR ROAD, NALLASOPARA (W), MUMBAI, MAHARASHTRA - 401203. INDIAN
3.	Nature of the applicant's interest in the copyright of the work	:	AUTHOR
4.	Class and description of the work	:	LITERARY / BOOK
5.	Title of the work	:	ENGLISH WORD POWER
6.	Language of the work	:	ENGLISH
7.	Name, address and nationality of the author and if the author is deceased, date of his decease	:	NIRANJAN JHA SHOWMAN, CROMOSYS PUBLICATION, 001, JAYSATYAM, PATANKAR ROAD, NALLASOPARA (W), MUMBAI, MAHARASHTRA - 401203. INDIAN
8.	Whether the work is published or unpublished	:	UNPUBLISHED
9.	Year and country of first publication and name, address and nationality of the publisher	:	N.A.
10.	Years and countries of subsequent publications, if any, and names, addresses and nationalities of the publishers	:	N.A. SAME AS ABOVE
11.	Names, addresses and nationalities of the owners of various rights comprising the copyright in the work and the extent of rights held by each, together with particulars of assignments and licences, if any	:	
12.	Names, addresses and nationalities of other persons, if any, authorised to assign or licence of rights comprising the copyright	:	N.A.
13.	If the work is an 'Artistic work', the location of the original work, including name, address and nationality of the person in possession of the work. (In the case of an architectural work, the year of completion of the work should also be shown).	:	N.A.
14.	If the work is an 'Artistic work', whether it is registered under the Designs Act 2000 if yes give details.	:	N.A.
15.	If the work is an 'Artistic work', capable of being registered as a design under the Designs Act 2000.whether it has been applied to an article though an industrial process and ,if yes ,the number of times it is reproduced.	:	N.A.
16.	Remarks, if any	:	

Diary Number :   7396/2019-CO/L
Date of Application : 09/05/2019
Date of Receipt :   09/05/2019

DEPUTY REGISTRAR OF COPYRIGHTS